More Praise for *The Inspiring Leader*

"The Inspiring Leader *demystifies the attributes of inspiration and how critical inspiration is to leader effectiveness and organization outcomes.*"

—PAUL MADSEN, Senior Director, HR & OD, Merck & Co., Inc.

"*With thorough and compelling research, the authors demystify inspiration and demonstrate that it is the most powerful leadership ingredient. They then provide simple and actionable methods that, when practiced, will take you down the path toward inspirational leadership.*"

—PAUL HOFFMAN, Vice President Human Resources, Hunt Consolidated, Inc.

"The Inspiring Leader *doesn't disappoint. [It reveals] that the key to being an extraordinary leader lies in unlocking inspiration and passion in yourself and your team.*"

—COURTNEY ROGERS, Executive Director, Human Resources, Amgen, Inc.

"*This is not a 'trust us we know' kind of leadership book. It is steeped in research and in the many combined years of experience that the authors draw on to make their points. The stories and examples they provide are excellent anecdotes that make their theory come to life.*"

—BEVERLY KAYE, Founder/CEO, Career Systems International, and coauthor of Love 'Em or Lose 'Em: Getting Good People to Stay

"*A refreshing and provocative read which I will add to my short list of 'must-read' for aspiring leaders.*"

—DAVID ROSSITER, Head of Human Resources, Hospital Authority of Hong Kong

THE
INSPIRING
LEADER

THE
INSPIRING
LEADER

UNLOCKING THE SECRETS
OF HOW EXTRAORDINARY
LEADERS MOTIVATE

**JOHN H. ZENGER | JOSEPH R. FOLKMAN
AND SCOTT K. EDINGER**

New York   Chicago   San Francisco   Lisbon   London   Madrid
Mexico City   Milan   New Delhi   San Juan   Seoul
Singapore   Sydney   Toronto

2 3 4 5 6 7 8 9 0   DOC/DOC   0 1 0 9

ISBN   978-0-07-162124-3
MHID   0-07-162124-5

The 360-degree feedback instrument referenced in this work, including each of the items and the language used to describe them, are copyrighted by the Zenger Folkman company and may not be used without specific permission.

Throughout the book, the authors have purposefully used gender-neutral, plural pronouns in an effort to be inclusive of all readers.

McGraw-Hill books are available at special quantity discounts to use as premiums and sales promotions, or for use in corporate training programs. To contact a representative please visit the Contact Us pages at www.mhprofessional.com.

This book is printed on acid-free paper.

Library of Congress Cataloging-in-Publication Data

Zenger, John H.

The inspiring leader: unlocking the secrets of how extraordinary leaders motivate / by John H. Zenger, Joseph R. Folkman, and Scott K. Edinger.
   p. cm.
   ISBN 0-07-162124-5 (alk. paper)
1. Leadership.   2. Employee motivation.   I. Folkman, Joe.   II. Title.
   HD57.7.Z464 2009
   658.4'092—dc22

                                                    2008050319

We dedicate this book to our colleagues and clients. Not only do our colleagues make the organization run smoothly, but they also are the genesis of countless first-class ideas. We could not ask for a more dedicated group with whom to work.

Our firm exists to serve clients, who often become good friends. They repeatedly challenge us to create new solutions that, without their prodding, would never have been considered. Better yet, they regularly stretch our thinking.

Together our colleagues and clients are our greatest source of inspiration, and for that we are extremely grateful.

Contents

Foreword

IS *THE INSPIRING LEADER* FOR YOU?

Drs. Jack Zenger and Joe Folkman, along with their colleague Scott Edinger, have taken the study of leadership to a new level. I have the highest respect for them. Rather than just sharing "platitudes" about effective leadership based upon anecdotal data—or making "inferences" about effective leadership based upon studies involving college students—they have actually conducted research on leadership effectiveness involving over 200,000 respondents who work with *real* leaders in *real* organizations.

As a result of their extensive research, Jack, Joe, and Scott have concluded that *inspiration* is the most powerful of all leadership competencies in terms of being: 1) the best predictor of overall ratings of leadership effectiveness by direct reports, peers, and managers, 2) the quality most valued by employees, and 3) the factor most correlated with employee commitment and satisfaction.

The Inspiring Leader shares *why* inspiring leadership matters and *what* inspiring leadership means to staff members. More important, it goes on to describe *how* you can become a more inspiring leader.

In my role as an executive educator and coach, my mission is to help successful leaders achieve positive, lasting change in behavior for themselves, their people, and their teams. As I have grown older, I am no longer interested in just helping leaders *learn*—I am interested in helping leaders *do*. The world will not become a better place because you read this book and learn some interesting concepts. The world will become a better place because you apply what you have learned and do what Jack, Joe, and Scott suggest. This stuff has been proven. It works! But it only works if you do it. Let me illustrate this point with an example from one of my coaching clients.

Mary, one of the greatest CEOs that I have ever met, was talking with her potential successor, Rob. She was sharing some feedback on his recent inappropriate leadership behavior in a team meeting.

"Does this mean that I have to watch what I say—and worry about how I act—in every meeting for the *rest of my career*?" Rob, the potential CEO grumbled.

"Welcome to my world!" Mary sighed. If you ever want to become a CEO, get used to it. People are going to be listening to what you say—and watching how you act—in every meeting for the rest of your career."

If you truly want to become an inspiring leader, face the reality that the people you are leading will be listening to what *you* say—and watching how *you* act—in every meeting for the rest of your career.

The Inspiring Leader is a wonderful guidebook that can help you learn what to say—and how to act—in a manner that will inspire the people you are leading.

Inspiring leaders communicate with more than content. They communicate with emotion. Leadership is not just about the words you say—it is also about the emotions you convey. One reason that I love this book is that it goes beyond content of leadership communication and deals with the emotion of leadership communication.

As a leader, you may be sitting in an incredibly boring PowerPoint presentation, watching material that you have already read. You will still need to convey interest and caring. You are the leader. Your direct reports, who have developed this presentation, may have spent months of effort in preparation. They are looking at your face to gauge your reaction. While nonverbal signs of boredom or lack of caring can destroy their inspiration, nonverbal signs of pride and caring can increase their inspiration. As a leader, the difference will be up to you!

Being an inspiring leader is a choice. It is not easy. From my experience, the inspiring leaders described in this book are there for a reason. They earned it! The ideas presented herein will not be difficult to understand—they will be hard to do.

If you are willing to provide the caring, courage, and discipline needed to be an inspiring leader, this book can be a great asset. If you are not willing to provide these things, don't bother reading any further.

This book provides a wonderful road map. If you are willing to "pay the price"—use it as a guide on your leadership journey.

—Marshall Goldsmith
New York Times bestselling author of
What Got You Here Won't Get You There

Chapter 1

Inspiration: The Most Important Leadership Ingredient

The essence of leadership is that you can't blow an uncertain trumpet.

—Theodore M. Hesburgh

Leadership is based on a spiritual quality, the power to inspire others to follow.

—Vince Lombardi

Anyone who has worked in an organization for even a few years has witnessed a similar event. A group whose performance was flat and lackluster gets a new leader. Suddenly there's an excitement in the air. People are smiling. Productivity soars. What exactly makes this happen? Can more leaders learn to do this?

This book explains to leaders what they must do in order to bring about extraordinary performance by those they manage. It explains what is required to move a group that has been rather ho-hum to a state of being gung-ho. It tells what leaders do that breaks through the barrier of "just-get-by" mediocrity and enables them to lead their team to newfound heights of higher performance and profitability. It does this by focusing on an ingredient of leadership that has, for a variety of reasons, largely been ignored.

Books on leadership have invariably made the assumption that somehow leaders were able to influence the performance of their subordinates. However, depending on which book you read, the underlying reasons for that influence have been extremely varied.

For example, each book would attribute the result to a different factor, such as these:

- Brilliant strategic thinking
- Superb execution
- The leader's passion and strong drive for results
- Technical brilliance and innovation
- Strong interpersonal skills
- Nobility of character
- Being a good problem solver

The list goes on and on, given the thousands of books on the subject.

Yet, always in the background has been the recognition that part of the results that the leader produced may be coming from some poorly defined and described "secret sauce." In the past this has frequently been identified as "charisma." Somehow this ingredient was always recognized as being in the equation, but by its very nature, it seemed impossible to describe.

HOW IS THIS BOOK DIFFERENT?

Thousands of books have been written on the topic of leadership, and much of what is said comes from an opinion that gains popularity or the success stories of a single successful leader. This book is neither. We approach the topic of inspiration and motivation from an analytical perspective, using research methods with statistically significant data and objective empirical evidence regarding what makes a leader inspiring. As a result, this book is not a creation of ideas for how leaders inspire. Rather, it provides you with a discovery of what the best leaders around the world do to inspire and motivate others.

After all, what are leaders to do when they consider that their job requirements are to achieve financial objectives, meet organizational or divisional goals, implement changes, and manage teams of people, and while they are doing that, their bosses tell them to be sure to be inspirational and motivating?

The message of this book can be summed up this way. Leadership is very complex. It is made up of many components, several of which we've just noted. Like a wonderful dish served by a world-class chef, it has many ingredients that make it so delicious. While much has been written about many of the key ingredients, there is one that has received little attention, and yet it is the one that our research suggests is the most important.

The question, "What makes an outstanding leader?" has been asked many times. Our approach to attempting to find a valuable answer to that question came from having an extensive database that consisted of more than 200,000 multirater or 360-degree feedback instruments that described 20,000 managers. For several data sets inside that large database, we had company performance measures. This enabled us to identify those who received the highest aggregate scores and compare them with those who scored less well. By doing this, we were able to identify those competencies that most powerfully differentiated these different groups. Thus, our approach was empirical rather than clinical.

As time went on, we were frequently asked to identify which of these competencies was the "silver bullet" that made the greatest difference. It became increasingly clear that one of them, *"inspires and motivates to high performance,"* was the single most important quality or competency for the leader to possess. But let us reiterate: this does not mean that the other elements of leadership are not important. They can't be ignored.

This book will focus on the ingredient that has mostly been brushed over and forgotten. We'll attempt to explain why that may have happened, but beyond that, we will attempt to analyze it in a way that makes sense to the intelligent layman. Our most important objective, however, is to provide specific suggestions about how every leader can acquire more of this attribute.

This book is not completely unique in its focus on inspiration or charisma.[1] Others have alluded to this ingredient, but we come at this topic from a different perspective. We bring an empirical, analytical approach to this subject that would seem more likely to be applied by a poet or novelist. Our objective will be to demystify it and take it from the realm of an intangible, indefinable quality to something that can be studied and then put into practice. Our desire is to help leaders understand how they can better develop this quality and immediately put it to work in their daily leadership behavior.

WHY WE CHOSE THIS TOPIC

First, why did we choose this topic? The short answer is that after doing research for our earlier book, *The Extraordinary Leader*, we continued to analyze those competencies that were most powerful in separating extraordinary leaders from all the others. We had often been asked, "So if I have to choose one thing to work on, what should it be?" For a considerable time we avoided answering that question, because there were many leadership competencies that our research showed to be important. The easiest answer was the classic, "It depends." What people choose to work on should depend on their job, the company culture, the organization's strategic direction, their passion, and their interests.

As time went on, however, our research revealed that there was one leadership competency that deserved some special attention. It was "inspires and motivates to high performance." Three distinct pathways each led to this same conclusion.

1. First, our research showed "inspires and motivates to high performance" to be the most powerful predictor of someone's being seen as an extraordinary leader. From a field of 16 such competencies, this one clearly stood out.

   The specific measures that we used to describe this characteristic and that most powerfully made that separation of best and worst leaders were the following:
   a. "Inspires others to high levels of effort and performance."[©]
   b. "Energizes people to achieve exceptional results."[©]
2. Next, when the subordinates of tens of thousands of leaders were directly asked what leadership competency they most

wanted to have in their leader, their resounding first choice was "inspires and motivates to high performance."

3. Finally, when we measured employee commitment and engagement in organizations and analyzed what leadership behaviors were most associated with the highest levels of employee commitment, "inspires and motivates" again was the competency at the top of the list. It was consistently the most highly correlated with those employees who would recommend the organization to a friend, seldom thought about leaving, and were willing to go the extra mile.

We're not suggesting that there is a single "silver bullet" for leadership. But the ability of leaders to inspire those about them comes the closest to being that all-powerful solution. We simply cannot overemphasize how robust and dominant it is.

WHY MOTIVATION MATTERS

The authors have backgrounds that on the face of it would seem to make it unlikely that they would write a book on inspiration. Why? Because inspiration is a topic that most people see as "soft" and "mysterious," and nothing in our past work experience would point in this direction. In addition to that, our past research interests would also make us unlikely candidates for this topic.[2] We have a reputation for taking an empirical, relatively hard-nosed view of leadership and how leaders can best be developed. We insist on showing the business case for what we recommend. Frankly, in the past we gravitated away from the "touchy-feely" activities that were prevalent in our profession and favored the well-researched behavioral approach to developing leaders. We insist on doing only those things that have been proven to have a positive impact and really work.

Yet the reason we chose this subject is embedded in what has just been said. We could no longer simply ignore the topic just because it seems so hard to define or implement. That's a rather cowardly thing to do. Nor could we brush it under the carpet on the grounds that it is just too "squishy." That fact did not dissuade highly esteemed research psychologists like Martin Seligman from study-ing "happiness" or "optimism."

The compelling force that we could not escape was the simple fact that the data led us here. The empirical evidence confirms that there is a powerful dimension of leadership that strongly influences all leaders' performance and that had been evaded for far too long. It could be described as leadership development's "elephant on the table." You can pretend it isn't there, but everyone strongly suspects or knows it is there, despite the fact that few want to talk about it.

IS THIS BOOK FOR YOU?

This book is written for leaders in business, public-sector organiza-tions, health-care institutions, and educational institutions. The con-clusions are as relevant to long-established manufacturing companies as they are to a recent high-tech start-up. While the underlying data from which these conclusions are drawn come largely from North America, we have conducted enough studies in Latin America, Europe, the Middle East, and Asia-Pacific countries to be comfortable that these conclusions apply globally. Despite how much has been writ-ten about how different generations respond to leaders, our research showed no discernible conclusions indicating differences between baby boomers and the younger Gen-Xers, Gen-Yers, Millennials, or Nexters in this matter of how leaders inspire. It is cross-generational.

The only difference between "inspires and motivates to high performance" and what is more broadly described as influence is the target audience. In this book, we focus on the relationship of leaders with those who report to them, but exactly the same concepts and principles can apply to any individual's relationship with peers, customers, and suppliers. Furthermore, beyond work-ing relationships inside organizations, we submit that these find-ings are relevant to anyone who is attempting to influence other people in any situation. Therefore, these findings can be helpful to Boy and Girl Scout leaders, not-for-profit organizations, volun-teer leaders, and mothers and fathers.

A QUICK EXERCISE

Think of your own experience with different leaders with whom
you've interacted. It should be easy to identify those who were
basically competent and effective. In the left-hand column, under
the heading "Competent Leader," jot down the names of three
leaders whom you've known well. Choose three who were competent but not extraordinary. Choose ones who were technically competent, smart, and hard-working and who kept the organization's
interests above their own. Let's assume that your list of competent
leaders represents people with no major defects. Chances are that
these people gave clear direction, followed up on assignments, were
considerate of others, and acted with integrity. They were competent, but there was no inspiration. Typically, people respond to this
kind of leader by doing their jobs and completing their assignments, but they don't do much extra.

Competent Leader   **Extraordinary Leaders**

_____   _____

_____   _____

_____   _____

Then, under the heading "Extraordinary Leaders," contrast
those leaders with three others who truly inspired you. Think of
people whose leadership caused you to put forth extra effort, to be
extremely creative, and to be doggedly persistent. Think of when
work felt like it was a "cause" or a "calling," and you smile when
you think about it. In the right-hand column, list those three leaders who inspired you to perform at your peak.

These leaders somehow motivated you to do more than you
expected you could. Whatever you were doing seemed like a "cause,"
rather than a job or an assignment. Work was something that you
wanted to do rather than something that you *had* to do. You
were clear about your goals, and you had a burning desire to be

successful. Those around you were also caught up in the excitement. Everyone was working hard to make something important happen.

There is a dramatic difference between the two experiences. We've noticed that people invariably smile when they talk about their experience with the leaders in the right-hand column. They seldom smile when they talk about their experience with those on the left. Adequate leaders get everyone to do their jobs, but inspirational leaders are able to get people to rise far above that mark and achieve more. They perform better on an individual basis, and the team they work in performs better as well.

Now think about your current situation. Which describes the kind of leadership that you provide? If you have subordinates, do they consistently go the extra mile? Do they take complete responsibility, act with optimism and enthusiasm, bounce back when things go poorly, and in general act like owners rather than hired hands? Do people laugh and appear to be having a good time at work?

If you would like to have more of that behavior from the people who report to you, then we invite you to read on. We think you will find some valuable ideas about making that happen.

WHY WE'VE AVOIDED THIS TOPIC IN THE PAST

We think there are many reasons why this topic of "charisma" or "inspiration" has been skirted for so long.

1. It is hard to define and quantify.
2. It is on the "softer" side of the so-called soft skills.
3. It has not been clear that there were measurable business consequences.

Let's explore each of these reasons briefly.

Inspiration Is Hard to Define and Quantify

The word *inspiration* literally means "putting life into something that had been lifeless." It is the concept involved in the biblical account of God putting spirits into the bodies of Adam and Eve in order that they might have life. While many books have been written about motivation, little has been written about inspiration. Even less has been written that is based on any research. That's what we believe separates the information in this book from much of what you might have read in the past. Fortunately, some good researchers have begun to explore the topic. We're grateful to them because their work begins to provide some answers.

We have also associated this dimension of inspirational leadership with the term *charisma*. It has been a catchall phrase to describe all those qualities and behaviors that could not be defined and measured, but that obviously had a strong impact on the results that a leader produced. *Charis* means "grace" or "gift" in Greek, and it has come to be associated with a special gift or power displayed by a leader. The sociologist Max Weber described it as "a certain quality of an individual personality by virtue of which he is set apart from ordinary men and treated as endowed with supernatural, superhuman, or at least specifically exceptional powers or qualities."[3] For more than 60 years, astute observers have noted this unique dimension of leaders, but it has been left in the category of questions that someone jokingly described as "too hard."

Be aware that we will use the terms *charisma* and *inspiration* somewhat interchangeably as we go forward. Based on our analysis, they seem extremely close to each other. We realize that some think of charisma as being a broad collection of qualities that creates a leader's influence. However, the same can be said of inspiration. Some may think of inspiration as being a bit narrower and linked to specific actions. We've chosen to make them virtually equal.

> Together the terms *inspiration* and *charisma* feel as if they are in the same category as the word *pornography*. We have all heard the classic comment by Judge Black, who acknowledged: "I can't define it, but I can recognize it when I see it." That's how most have approached charisma and inspiration, and this is where we seem to be at the moment.

It Is on the "Softer" Side of the So-Called Soft Skills

Possibly because it has been hard to define, social scientists have shied away from motivation as a topic for analysis on the grounds that if the topic of interpersonal skills was a soft subject, this was simply over the top. A few academics have attempted to define it, but virtually no progress has been made on how to develop it.[4] Until recently, any work done in the way of practical attempts to help leaders develop these qualities has been in the hands of people from the world of drama and acting[5] or that of presentation skills training.

This topic switches from the more cognitive, rational, and potentially empirical analysis of observable behavior over to another side. It is now in the realm of emotions, feelings, affect, and energy. It is a territory where many of us begin to squirm and become extremely uncomfortable. Yes, most of us can intellectually acknowledge that feelings are important, but the traditional businessperson tends to leave that world for the actors, artists, singers, poets, and painters to tend. It is a realm that we don't pretend to understand well, let alone know how to help others develop. Most students of leadership dimly see it and acknowledge its importance, and it is into that world that we will attempt to usher you. It is also the world into which we hope to bring more light.

It Has Not Been Clear That There Were Measurable Business Consequences

When dealing with groups of executives, we have been surprised by the number who don't see much of a direct link between leadership effectiveness and organizational performance. We don't have precise data on this question, but it seems as if about 40 percent of the leaders we encounter don't see that direct linkage between leadership and business results. The good news is that the majority see the connection. The telling fact, however, is this: if the business impact of overall leadership excellence is not clear, then it is very clear that a leader's ability to inspire others would not be seen as having powerful business consequences.

HOW THE REST OF THE BOOK IS ORGANIZED

Chapter 2 summarizes our research on the link between leadership and business outcomes, and, specifically, on the linkage between inspiration and business results.

Chapter 3 explains the objectives for leaders' inspiring behavior. Leadership is obviously directed to subordinates, peers, and those elsewhere in the firm. But, for what purpose? To what end? This chapter defines what the inspirational leader actually accomplishes and why that is so important to the organization.

Chapter 4 provides a quick overview of the research that underpins this work. We didn't want any reader to get bogged down in a somewhat detailed discourse on research, so we've presented only what we thought you needed to know in order to fully appreciate that these conclusions are on a solid footing.

Chapter 5 describes some general characteristics or attributes that the inspirational leader needs to possess. Such compelling data existed for the importance of these basic attributes that we concluded that the reader needed to understand them and their importance for her success. For those who may not have those attributes fully developed, we offer some useful suggestions.

Chapters 6 through 12 are the heart of the book. If your reading time is limited, go there. They present the research that shows precisely what leaders do that inspires the people about them. We have attempted to make this as operational and actionable as possible. A big complaint about books of this kind has been that they serve up platitudes that are nearly impossible for an average mortal to put into action.

Chapter 13 approaches this topic from the opposite direction. What do we know about leaders who have just the opposite effect from being inspirational? What precisely do these leaders do? Can we apply those lessons to ourselves to ensure that we aren't guilty of these practices that do not inspire, but rather have the opposite effect?

Chapter 14 presents our final conclusions and summarizes our findings. You may obtain a copy of this to keep in a convenient place for frequent reference by going to www.zengerfolkman.com/ Products/Inspiring Leader/summary. There you will also find other helpful tools and information.

Finally, be prepared to be reminded of important concepts. Don't expect startling revelations of new truth. The big secret is that there is no big secret. Many of the actions of leaders that inspire others are simply wise management and leadership practices that have been described by others. When we work with leaders, we occasionally hear, "This is common sense." That is true. Our response is simply, "Unfortunately, not often enough is it common practice." There is a chasm between knowing what you should do and doing it. Ask anyone who has ever been on a diet. Our contribution may simply be to make you keenly aware of how important those actions are to your success in inspiring those about you. If you'd like further information and resources about the ideas in this book go to www.zengerfolkman and click on the Inspiring Leader icon.

Part 1

The Importance of Inspiration

T he first section of this book explains why, out of all the topics that make up the broad subject of leadership, we chose this topic. We believe you'll find this both interesting and important, but you could move directly to Part 2, "The Making of an Inspirational Leader." Here's what you'd miss.

Chapter 2 has a simple message: inspiration makes sense from a hard-nosed business perspective. Inspiration affects several business outcomes that most executives care about, and this chapter presents the evidence.

Chapter 3 flips the subject of inspirational leadership upside down and looks at it from the perspective of the subordinates. What exactly is the impact of inspirational leaders on the people they lead? What do we want to see happening with that group? Isn't looking at the behavior of their subordinates the best way to assess whether leaders are truly inspirational?

Chapter 4 presents a brief description of the research methodology that led us to our conclusions. We've saved some of the details for Appendix 1 and have done our best to keep this chapter mercifully short. However, your acceptance and understanding of our conclusions hinges on a basic understanding of how we came to these findings.

Chapter 2

The Business Outcomes of Inspiration

Outstanding leaders go out of their way to boost the self-esteem of their people. If people believe in themselves it's amazing what they can accomplish.

—Sam Walton

In the previous chapter, we briefly described our research finding that inspiring others was the most powerful predictor of being an extraordinary leader, that inspiring others was rated as the most important competency of leaders, and that inspiring others was also the best predictor of having direct reports who are satisfied with and committed to their jobs. After discovering this information, we researched the impact that inspirational leaders have on important outcomes. Our most recent analysis focused on a dataset of almost 8,110 leaders from more than 100 different organizations as rated by 41,436 direct reports.

First, we isolated the effectiveness of these leaders on just one competency: *inspiring others*. We then divided these leaders into five groups in terms of their ability to inspire others based on the ratings of their direct reports. The five groups included:

- Bottom 10 percentiles
- Eleventh through thirty-fifth percentiles
- Thirty-sixth through sixty-fifth percentiles
- Sixty-sixth through ninetieth percentiles
- Top 10 percentiles

Each leader's direct reports were also asked a series of questions to assess their overall level of satisfaction with and commitment to the organization. We wanted to understand their intention to leave the organization, their willingness to recommend the organization to others, and their confidence that the organization would achieve its goals.

The results of this analysis revealed a highly consistent trend. Figure 2-1 shows the percentile score on the overall satisfaction and commitment of direct reports, segmented by which percentile grouping the leader fell into in the rating on *inspires others*.

We see in the figure that leaders who were ineffective when it comes to inspiring and motivating others (tenth percentile or lower) ended up having very dissatisfied and uncommitted employees (on average, they scored at the twenty-sixth percentile on the Employee Satisfaction/Commitment Index). There is a clear trend demonstrating that the more effective leaders were at inspiring and motivating others, the more satisfied their direct reports were, and the more committed they were to the organization overall.

To test the cultural and industry consistency of the results, this same analysis was applied to companies in a variety of industries (e.g., manufacturing, high tech, financial services, oil, and hospitals), and

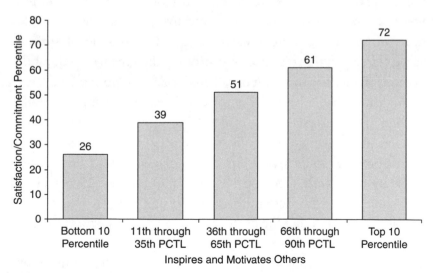

Figure 2-1 Employee Satisfaction/Commitment Percentile

the same trend emerged. We then looked at results from a financial services firm in India and a division of government employees in the United Arab Emirates. The trend was the same.

The impact of inspiring and motivating others is very consistent across different kinds of organizations and within different cultures. We found that leaders who were skilled at inspiring and motivating others tended to have direct reports who were more satisfied and committed overall.

INTENTION TO LEAVE

Organizations are beginning to feel the impact of the 76 million members of the baby-boom generation who are preparing for retirement in the next 5 to 10 years. The pool of talent to replace those who are retiring is substantially smaller, by some 20 million, and the resulting high demand and low supply highlight the need to understand more about what it takes to retain employees. We studied the impact that leaders who were highly effective at inspiring and motivating others would have on employee retention.

Using the same data set of over 8,000 leaders, and again isolating the effectiveness of these leaders on just one competency, *inspires others*, we divided them into the same five percentile groups. This time, direct reports were asked to respond on a scale of strongly agree, agree, neutral, disagree, and strongly disagree to the question, "I rarely think about quitting my job and going to another company."

We found that at least half of the employees reporting to a leader scoring in the lowest 10 percentiles think about quitting their jobs. Leaders in the second percentile segment from the top (sixty-sixth to ninetieth percentiles) face only about one in four employees who think about quitting. The top 10 percentiles had just 19 percent of their employees who were thinking about quitting (see Figure 2-2). We also discovered that the percentage of employees who responded neutrally or negatively to this question correlated with actual turnover. Typically about 50 percent of the people who think about quitting actually end up leaving the organization.

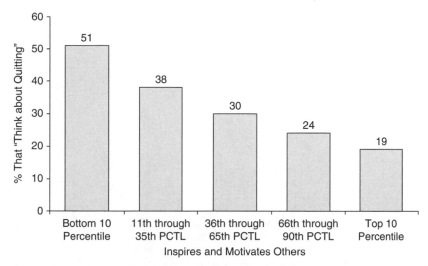

Figure 2-2 Percent of Employees Who "Think about Quitting"

HIGHLY COMMITTED EMPLOYEES

In a third study using the same data set, we looked at the extent to which an inspirational leader would affect the percentage of direct reports that are highly committed. Occasionally everyone encounters an employee who is what we might refer to as "gung ho." A gung-ho direct report approaches work with a great deal of enthusiasm, is always willing to take on difficult assignments, will do whatever is necessary in order to succeed, and looks for opportunities to do more than is expected. Such employees are highly valued and appreciated. In our research, we have found that these employees exist in every organization. Between 10 and 15 percent of employees behave this way regardless of the work environment. However, leaders greatly influence the percentage of highly committed employees in their work group. Figure 2-3 shows the average percentage of highly committed employees based on the effectiveness of a leader at inspiring her direct reports.

It is clear from Figure 2-3 that the more effective a leader is at inspiring and motivating others, the higher the percentage of employees that are highly committed. And for those leaders who

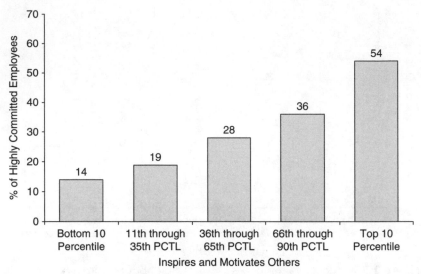

Figure 2-3 Percent of Highly Committed Employees

truly excel at motivating and inspiring, over half of their work team behaves this way. What kind of impact do you think that has on the other half? We often ask leaders about the impact of having a large percentage of highly committed employees in their work group. Their response is very consistent. It affects everything—productivity, the ability of the team to get projects done on time, and the willingness of less motivated employees to work hard.

Peter Drucker made the observation that if most businesses increased the productivity of employees by only 10 percent, they would double their profits. When most people first hear this statement, they are skeptical, but once they consider the fixed cost of their employees and the company's profit margin, most of them agree that Drucker was correct. Their observation is, "That small increase in productivity all goes to the bottom line, and it doesn't cost the company anything."

As you consider Drucker's statement and the impact that inspirational leaders have on the percentage of highly committed employees, it is not hard to assume that having a higher percentage of highly committed employees would ultimately affect profitability.

Some people have asked the question, "What about those employees who are not highly committed? How are they affected by the highly committed?"

Most people can relate to the following example, which explains what usually happens.

> When you are jogging, walking, or bike riding and someone passes you, what do you do? For most people, the answer is always the same: they speed up. The reality is that if over half of the employees on your team are highly committed, the remainder of the team will not be too far behind.

We conducted an additional study on the *impact of inspiration on productivity.*

Employees were assessed on their perceptions of the productivity in their work group. They also rated their immediate manager on inspiration. The five items assessing productivity are as follows:

1. In my business unit or department, we are striving to continually improve work processes, procedures, and work flows to enhance overall productivity.
2. Conditions in my job allow me to be as productive as I can be.
3. In my business unit or department, there is very little wasted time because people can be productive without delays or distractions.
4. Meetings I attend are a productive use of my time.
5. My business unit or department is run efficiently.

Figure 2-4 shows the results of this study.

This particular study showed us the impact that leaders with even modest levels of inspiration can have. Note that leaders in the middle 30 percent have substantially higher positive responses on the productivity index.

INSPIRATIONAL LEADERS ACHIEVE MORE

As you review these studies, the conclusions are obvious. Leaders who know how to inspire others have higher levels of employee

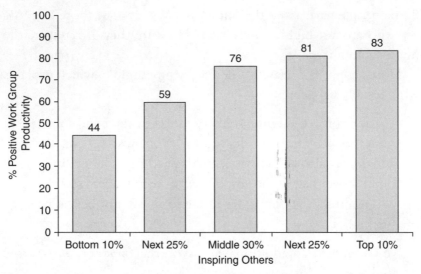

Figure 2-4 Percent of Positive Responses on Work Group Productivity

satisfaction and commitment, much better retention, and a sub-stantially larger percentage of highly committed employees. We did additional studies and found the same trend for a variety of other outcomes. We were frankly surprised that just one area of compe-tence would have so much influence.

CASE STUDY ON THE IMPACT OF INSPIRATION

After collecting data on more than 100 high-potential leaders, the company profile became very clear. The leaders in this organization were very competent. One of their strongest competencies was driv-ing for results. One of the senior leaders in the organization fondly described this competency as "push." When the profile of these leaders was further examined, we found that this group was sub-stantially less effective at inspiring others. This competency was referred to as "pull." When looking at these data, one senior leader said, "Perhaps we need a little less push and a little more pull." In our opinion, that was the wrong solution. To provide evidence for our recommendation, we did the following analysis.

We examined the results from the company and looked at those leaders who scored above the seventy-fifth percentile on inspiring others but below the seventy-fifth percentile on drive for results. We found that 11 percent of the leaders who were rated as extraordinary (at the ninetieth percentile overall) had that profile. Then we looked at those leaders who scored above the seventy-fifth percentile on drive for results but below the seventy-fifth percentile on inspiring others. We found 17 percent. When you looked at each competency individually, neither was that impressive. We then looked at leaders who were above the seventy-fifth percentile on both inspiring others and driving for results. The combined effect of doing both well was that 73 percent were rated at the ninetieth percentile (see Figure 2-5).

This is a powerful example of the power of the interaction effect with competencies. Think of the person who is trying to lose weight. Healthy eating is part of the formula, but when this is combined with a good exercise regimen, the person will lose weight two to three times faster and is more likely to sustain the weight loss. Doing one or the other is a good thing. Doing both creates a far greater result.

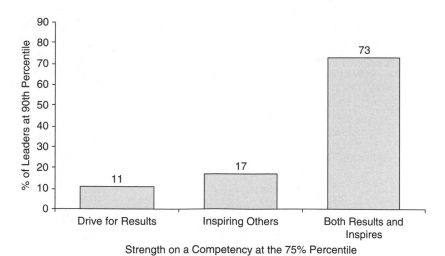

Figure 2-5 Percent of Extraordinary Leaders

This case study teaches a very important lesson: while inspiring others is a very critical competency, the true impact of this skill is substantially greater when it is enhancing another competency. Instead of "less push and more pull," what this company needed was more push combined with more pull. The effect of these two competencies together created enormous synergy. As we suggested earlier, inspiring others is much like an excellent seasoning that brings out the flavors of your favorite foods.

CONCLUSION

The research confirms the impact of inspiring others. Leaders who are effective at inspiring others have employees who are more satisfied and committed. Such leaders are better able to retain employees, especially their highly committed employees.

Chapter 3

How Inspired Colleagues Behave

A leader is a dealer in hope.

—Napoleon Bonaparte

If people are coming to work excited,
If they're making mistakes freely and fearlessly,
If they're having fun,
If they're concentrating on doing things rather than
preparing reports and going to meetings,
Then somewhere you have leaders.

—Robert Townsend

The philosopher Johann Wolfgang von Goethe wrote an amazingly insightful description of leadership. In it he said:

> I have come to the frightening conclusion that I am the decisive element.
> It is my personal approach that creates the climate.
> It is my daily mood that makes the weather.
> I possess tremendous power to make a life miserable or joyous.
> I can be a tool of torture or an instrument of inspiration.
> I can humiliate or humor, hurt or heal.

Goethe eloquently captured leaders' power to influence the attitudes and feelings of their colleagues. He zeroes in on the fact that the leader creates the overall climate of the organization and on how the leader's shifting moods bring sunshine or frostbite to those about them. Goethe recognized that while all emotions are highly contagious, the leader's mood is especially powerful. It becomes a zephyr of cheer and happiness or a chilling breeze of darkness and gloom.

We noted earlier that the ultimate test of leadership should be how the leader's colleagues behave. That is, after all, what leadership is all about, and if you want to know how leaders ought to lead, you need to pay attention to those who are led. However, nearly everything written on the subject of leadership talks exclusively about what the leader should be or know or do differently. The focus is nearly always squarely on the leader, not the subordinates. We think this leaves out an important part of the equation. Leadership has a purpose and an expected outcome. The question to be asked is: "What has changed in the behavior of those being led?" One important dimension of becoming a better leader is to be clear about the outcomes you seek from those you lead.

Several streams of research are relevant to this question. It is hard to select from the many possibilities and desirable outcomes that could be included, but we have attempted to select those that have been shown to truly make a significant difference.

PRODUCTIVITY

One outcome that we seek from a leader's inspiration and motivation is that subordinates work more efficiently, that they produce more, and that what they produce has higher quality. To accomplish this, they work with greater speed and efficiency. As a result, there is less waste. In short, they are simply more productive.

Research conducted by Hunter, Schmidt, and Judiesch documented the huge differences in productivity among people occupying the same kind of position. Figure 3-1 summarizes that research.[1]

Those who work in large organizations know that the two people in a medium-complexity job who are at the extreme ends of

Wide Variations in Personal Productivity
Low-Complexity Jobs

• The top person is 3 times more
  productive than the bottom person,
  and 1.5 times more productive than
  the person at the 50th percentile.

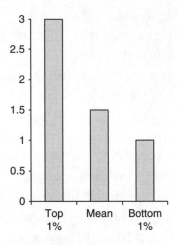

Wide Variations in Personal Productivity
Medium-Complexity Jobs

• The top person is 12 times
  more productive than the bottom
  person, and 2.7 times more
  productive than the person at
  the 50th percentile.

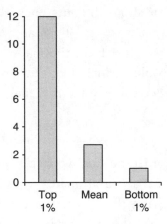

Figure 3-1 Differences in Productivity

the bell-shaped curve are making widely different contributions to
the organization's success. The one at the top is, in fact, making 12
times the contribution of the one at the bottom, but that person's
monetary compensation is often the same as or only slightly different from that of the person at the bottom.

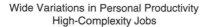

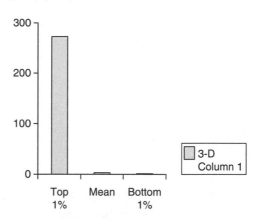

- The difference between the top 1% and the bottom 1% is so dramatic that statisticians say it can only be described as "infinite." The top person is 2.27 times more productive than the person at the 50th percentile.

Figure 3-1 (*continued*)

Leaving aside the differences between the top 1 percent and the bottom 1 percent, the gulf between the top person at the ninety-ninth percentile and the person who is squarely in the middle is also quite dramatic. For medium-complexity jobs, that top person is more than doubling the contribution of the person in the middle. Our point is that these differences are not to be sneezed at. Big opportunities exist. Leaders should do their best to improve the productivity of everyone because there is obviously such a long distance for many to go before they reach the highest possible level.

What is the role of the leader in encouraging those in the upper quartile to be so highly productive? Clearly some of a worker's effectiveness lies solely within himself. Maybe some of that is prewired and there from birth. Some of it is instilled by parents. We suggest that it is also strongly influenced by the person's leader and the environment that that leader creates. Earlier we presented data showing the correlation between employee engagement and the quality of the leader. Leaders do something that elicits more focused, more consistent, and more creative outcomes.

Anyone who has ridden on a Swiss train can't help marveling at the efficiency, the cleanliness, the on-time arrivals and departures, and the overall high level of productivity you experience on the trip. Is this the result of one specific leadership behavior? Obviously not. It begins with the leader caring about maintaining the Swiss tradition of punctuality and efficiency. It involves people putting forth great effort to correct anything that would disrupt the schedule, or to get back on schedule if there is a delay. The leader works to constantly improve the systems and processes. It is a host of things that every leader does that maintains this centuries-old tradition of excellence.

Productivity improvement is a convenient way of assessing whether or not a leader has been effective in influencing subordinates in a positive way. We wish to emphasize the importance of this outcome, as there is no question but that the leader plays an extremely crucial role in elevating the level of productivity in any organization. This is in part because the leader controls the processes that are being employed, which, in turn, have an enormous impact on the efficiency of every organization.

Frankly, we hesitated to list productivity first, primarily because one segment of our readers might already believe that this is the only important outcome of inspiration. This group would equate an inspired subordinate with one who produces more and ignore virtually everything else. We acknowledge the importance of productivity improvement, but we strongly argue that there are a number of other extremely important outcomes of inspiration. These other outcomes often contribute to higher levels of productivity, but they are extremely valuable in and of themselves.

CONFIDENCE

Organizations succeed when their people act with assurance and boldness. Jack Welch, former CEO of General Electric, frequently wrote and spoke of this need to drive self-confidence down into the organization. What creates such confidence?

Stanford University professor of psychology Albert Bandura, whose research is cited more frequently than that of any other living psychologist, has been a longtime researcher on self-efficacy and confidence. He suggests that this comes when people feel that there is a high likelihood of success when they attempt something new. Bandura wrote:

> People who have a strong belief in their capabilities think, feel and behave differently from those who have doubts about their capabilities. People who doubt their capabilities shy away from difficult tasks. They have low aspirations and weak commitments to the goals they choose to pursue. Failure wrecks their motivation. They give up quickly in the face of difficulties and are slow to recover their confidence following failure or setbacks.[2]

Simply put, unless people possess high feelings of confidence or self-efficacy, there simply is no performance. It is too risky, as they see it. Investing your energy is not worth it unless you have a strong belief that you will succeed.

Because of this, one of the healthiest attributes for people to have is an abiding belief that if they attempt something, they will succeed. This encourages people in every area of the organization to push forward and upward. It is an outcome of inspiration. A confident salesperson is willing to approach a challenging new account. A confident engineer agrees to find a better way to design a product. A confident accountant agrees to produce financial statements shortly after the month ends. Confident manufacturing employees agree to produce to an extremely high standard of quality that will satisfy the most demanding client. In every area of the firm, it is confidence that encourages people to try things that are new and challenging. The key question is: "What gives people that confidence?"

Bandura contends that this comes from having had success in similar activities in the past. It also comes when failed attempts have not been punished by the leader. Bandura's research on self-efficacy confirms that there are practical ways to enhance self-confidence. He suggests that the most powerful approaches are these:

1. Vicarious learning (behavior modeling)
2. Mental rehearsal
3. Experiencing increasingly challenging tasks
4. Feedback from respected others

Leaders make these four things happen in the following ways:

1. The leader can arrange for appropriate training that includes excellent examples of the proper way to do things. Such learning experiences are referred to as *behavior modeling* or *vicarious learning*. This is the best way to teach anything that has a skill component. What exactly is this?

   Teaching someone to play golf by reading a book is extremely difficult. Nothing compares to having someone stand nearby and explain the various clubs, then demonstrate how to hold the club, where to plant your feet, and how to take the right swing. Then the instructor asks you to do it and provides useful feedback on what you're doing, along with suggestions for how to do it better. Many jobs benefit from that same approach to learning, whether it is a salesperson being trained to relate to a prospect or a customer service rep talking on the phone with a client who has experienced some problem with your product.

   If a picture is worth a thousand words, then watching someone assemble a carburetor or remove an appendix is worth ten thousand words. Most people learn best by watching good examples and understanding why the example was selected. It also helps if the elements that are combined to make such a good example are identified so that the learner is clear about the important steps that are being demonstrated.

   Simply put, the most powerful way to give people a feeling of confidence and self-efficacy about their ability to perform some task is to teach them to do it very well and to let them know that their success was the result of their effort, persistence, and skill, not some uncontrollable external factors.

2. Leaders teach the value of mentally reviewing or rehearsing important events as a way to develop confidence. For years, sport psychologists have worked with professional athletes on the power of visualization as part of their preparation. The same practice can be applied effectively by many leaders. Confident people aren't embarrassed to rehearse important conversations with customers. They welcome the chance to practice the presentation they'll make to another department about the reasons for changing a work process.

3. Leaders build confidence by ensuring that people are given challenging assignments. When they delegate tasks, it isn't just through the filter of "Who can get the job done on time and on budget?" but with an eye to the question, "Who will benefit the most from this project?" or "Who really needs this to further his career development?"

4. Leaders should be a main source of feedback. Without exception, studies show that people at every level, from senior vice presidents to the mailroom clerk, want a good deal more feedback than they typically get. That difference between what they want and what they get is not small, it is huge. And yes, most people especially appreciate positive feedback, but most also want to learn how they can perform at a higher level and will welcome developmental feedback, so long as the message is delivered in a respectful, constructive manner.

   Feedback is especially helpful when it conveys, "You've almost got that right" or "You are 90 percent of the way there . . . just hang in there."

The bottom line is, the overall level of confidence that everyone has is part of the culture of an organization. Leaders are the driving force in creating that culture and the attendant positive emotions within people.

Self-efficacy has been shown to predict work-related performance more powerfully than more traditional performance-enhancement initiatives such as goal setting or measures of job satisfaction.[3]

OPTIMISM AND HOPE

Leaders shape the way people feel about the future in the broadest and most profound way. We readily acknowledge that this quality begins at a very deep level for most people. It starts with the most basic questions every human must face. Does life have any real purpose and meaning? Is there some reason for my being here? Hope is enhanced when there is a belief that life is purposeful and that people exist for some higher reason. For some people, that nets out to a simple, "I want to make a difference." Others see the opportunity to leave a lasting legacy.

In addition to having a broader view of the future, however, some people see the right side and the bright side of life in every dimension. A lot depends on what you are looking for. There is an old saying, "Seeing is believing." But there is an even more accurate saying that suggests, "Believing is seeing." We see what we're looking for and what we want to believe. Two people observing the exact same event can "see" very different things. Working in an organization in which people see the bright side is a night-and-day difference from being involved with those who can see only the dark side. Leaders strongly influence the degree to which people have optimism and hope regarding the future of the organization and their role in it.

This is an extremely important dimension. An abundance of research clearly confirms that those who have higher levels of optimism are significantly happier and healthier, enjoy greater success in their occupations, have more lasting and happy relationships, and make greater contributions to their communities.

If you define optimism and hope as being in a "good mood," Martin Seligman[4] reports that "adults and children who are put into a good mood select higher goals, perform better, and persist

longer on a variety of laboratory tests, such as solving anagrams."
He also muses about the relationship of overall happiness and productivity. Does high productivity cause happiness, or is it the other
way around? He concludes, "Research suggests ... that more happiness actually causes more productivity and higher income."[5]

Optimism can be learned and magnified through the practice of
several behaviors. These include focusing on the positive dimensions of life and expressing gratitude to others for their contributions to your life. For more, see Seligman's excellent treatise
Learned Optimism.[6]

> Seligman studied life insurance salespeople at
> Metropolitan Life Insurance Co. and discovered that
> although agents were normally selected on the basis of
> their scores on a long-established industry test, if a test
> that measured optimism was used, those agents who
> scored in the top half on this test of optimism actually
> outsold those who scored in the pessimistic half by 37
> percent. Agents who were in the top 10 percent on opti-
> mism outsold those in the bottom 10 percent on the
> same scale by 88 percent. The company then agreed to
> have a group of applicants take both the industry test and
> the optimism instrument. It then hired a "special force"
> made up of agents who had failed the industry test, but
> scored in the top half on the optimism instrument. The
> agents in this group sold as much as the optimistic agents
> who passed the industry test. They outsold the pessimistic
> agents who had passed the industry instrument by 21
> percent in their first year, and then outsold their pes-
> simistic counterparts by 57 percent in their second year.
> Seligman then found that among those who passed the
> industry test, optimists outsold pessimists by 8 percent in
> their first year and by 31 percent in their second year.
> Needless to say, the company opted to include a measure
> of optimism in its selection battery of tests.

INITIATIVE

The inspired and motivated employee does not wait to be told to do everything, but instead looks around, sees what needs to be done, and begins to do it. Initiative entails stepping in to rescue something that is about to fall into a crack between two departments. Initiative describes the mentality of an "owner" rather than a typical "hired hand."

Leaders create a culture in which people sense that this type of initiative will be rewarded, not punished. Doors have been opened. There is an emphasis on what people can do, not just on what they can't do. Peter Drucker once remarked that "much of what we call 'management' consists of a variety of things that make it difficult for the typical employee to do his job."

Employee handbooks go to great lengths to spell out the many things that can't be done, but they seldom include any description of those things that can be done. Worse yet, an employee who ventures out and tries something without getting explicit permission is often rebuked rather than being rewarded.

Initiative is difficult to teach. But what leaders can do is create a climate of freedom that allows people to experiment and also reward those who take the initiative. Leaders signal in many subtle ways whether initiative is welcomed or viewed with suspicion. One of the coauthors of this book, Jack Zenger, tells of this experience:

> An executive from a large San Francisco bank came by my hotel, picked me up, and took me to his office for a meeting we'd be holding in his building. We parked in the underground lot beneath the building. My friend mentioned, "You'll get a kick out of our garage attendant." So, I was on the alert to see what set this attendant apart from the norm. While most attendants greet customers with a nod or a grunt, this person was absolutely effusive. He greeted us by name and acted as if we were old high school classmates whom he hadn't seen in 20 years. He asked about our plans for the day so

that he'd know where best to park the car. He escorted us to the elevator bank, pressed the button to get an elevator car for us, and sent us on our way.

He had taken a job that some would see as being on the menial end of the spectrum and made it into a "calling." He injected himself into his work and brightened everyone's day in the process.

What distinguishes such people? They have the mentality to seek to do the most they can with their job, unlike the many who seek to do the least that is required. Leaders create the climate in which that behavior flourishes.

RESPONSIBLE BEHAVIOR

Another outcome that we should seek in those we lead is for people to act with a high level of responsibility. People with higher levels of motivation enjoy being held accountable for outcomes and don't place blame on others for any shortcomings in their own performance. Responsible people monitor and obtain information about their own and their group's performance. Responsible people identify strongly with the group to which they belong and always put organizational goals before any personal objectives. Responsible people do things for which there is no immediate personal reward, but which clearly benefit the welfare of the organization.

A culture of responsibility and accountability is created when leaders convey a strong message that the people at large and teams are what counts, and that leaders are there to do blocking and tackling for the employees.

In the recent spate of scandals involving senior executives, several of them have claimed, "I didn't know what was going on. I just signed the financial statements, and I was relying on my CFO." Wisely, it appears that most juries don't buy that foolishness.

Jack was an executive in a pharmaceutical firm that manufactured steroid chemicals in a plant in Mexico. The firm

decided to transfer all its manufacturing to a newly constructed plant in the Bahamas. Pilot plant operations had
been tested there and had worked. The Mexico facility
was closed, and the new plant scaled up its production.
However, for reasons that were unclear at the time, the
new plant was unable to produce an acceptable product
in sufficient volume to meet the firm's commitments to
its customers.

The CEO of the firm met with the assembled management team
and said, "We could blame a lot of people for what has happened. But
we all made this decision together. In hindsight, we should have been
smart enough to know that scaling up production was risky. I want to
take responsibility for this mistake. Now let's do all we can to fix it and
meet our customers' needs as best we can. But let's have no finger-
pointing at the people in our chemical production division."

When leaders own up to their mistakes, the pattern is established
for others to do the same thing.

ENTHUSIASM

Some people merely go through the motions. Others inject energy
and passion into what they do. Some people appear to deliberately
constrain their enthusiasm. We've realized for a long time that
enthusiasm and passion are the qualities that define the great performers in show business and athletics. It has been less clear that
this also holds true in more traditional organizations.

It also describes those workers who lift a position to a new level.

The Gallup organization has published a good deal about the
issue of employee engagement. According to its rather extensive
research, its best determination is that 29 percent of employees are
truly engaged in what they do. They enjoy their work and their colleagues and could be described as generally enthusiastic about their
daily occupation.

There is a much larger group, amounting to 55 percent of all
workers, who are not "engaged." They are blasé about what they

do. They lack enthusiasm, and it shows up in how they perform their work. These are the garage attendants who only nod or grunt when they see you. They are the retail clerks who only go through the motions, who don't suggest any "add-on" purchases, and who don't smile and look you in the eye as you check out and they hand you your receipt.

Finally, Gallup notes that 16 percent of all employees are actively disengaged. These are people who in subtle ways work at cross-purposes to their organization. They engage in internal sabotage that is estimated to cost the U.S. economy $350 billion annually.

Our research reinforces this conclusion. As part of a 360-degree feedback instrument, we ask direct reports of all leaders to indicate their level of employee engagement and commitment.

The analysis of our data from these questions reveals the general level of enthusiasm felt by a leader's subordinates. In the aggregate, we find that 14 percent of those surveyed have high levels of satisfaction and commitment. We define that as those who respond at the highest level on these questions. Below that, we have 40 percent who express moderate levels of enthusiasm for their organization and their work. That obviously leaves a large group of 46 percent who feel a lower level of enthusiasm for their work and for their organization.

Imagine what an organization would be like if 80 percent of its employees expressed a high level of enthusiasm regarding their work and the organization. We invite you to reflect for a moment on what would be different in your organization if that were true. Be as specific as you can about the impact of that on things that you already worry about—things such as retention, the ability to attract good people, the level of productivity, innovation and creativity, and levels of customer service.

The most promising approach to changing an emotion is to change behavior. When people learn to act in new ways, this clearly alters their inner feelings. People who learn to act with greater enthusiasm become more enthusiastic. Should you have any doubts about that concept, we invite you to try a quick experiment, providing it won't be too embarrassing. If you're sitting, slump forward, look at your feet for several seconds, put a gloomy expression on your face, and keep your knees together and your elbows close to your sides. Then try to sense how you "feel" inside. What's your mood when you do that?

Then, try the reverse. Sit up straight and tall as if you were a Marine sergeant. Smile. Look forward or up. Rehearse an important point that you might be making to some colleagues and gesture boldly. Now see what you identify as your strongest emotion. We predict that it will be moving toward the "enthusiasm" end of the scale rather than the "gloomy" end you were on before.

RESILIENCY

The ability to bounce back from an encounter with a barrier or hurdle is extremely important. This emotional "hardiness" means that barriers are seen as largely external, temporary, and surmountable. It begins with a willingness to accept reality and to work to improvise and adapt to your circumstances in order to achieve a goal.

Carol Dweck's research on mindsets confirms that people's reaction to challenging situations stems from a fundamental mindset, or point of view about life, that they have. She labels these mindsets as "proving" or "improving," and she argues that mindsets can be modified over time. Indeed, authority figures such as teachers and parents have a strong influence on children. It is clear that bosses in the organizations in which adults work take on this same power.

Dweck observes that parents often heap praise on a child, believing that this will enhance the child's self-esteem and feelings of worth. Messages like, "You're so smart" and "You are really intelligent" are made with very good intentions. But then the child's teacher gives her a particularly challenging math problem. She is stumped. Thoughts begin to flash through her mind: "Am I really stupid?" "Did Mom lie to me?" "Did I used to be smart and have I lost it?"

It would have been far better had the parent praised the child's hard work, tenacity, and ability to overcome obstacles that she encountered. Better that the parent say, "I really admire how persistent you've been in working on that report. You've put in lots of time and not let anything distract you." "I was glad to see that you found a way to get that additional information you needed to compete the report. That's a good example of how being resourceful pays off." Now when the child encounters an extremely challenging school assignment, she instantly says to herself, "I just need to work harder," or "I need to find a new approach to this problem."

The fact of the matter is that we all encounter challenges and difficulties. As the research on "derailed" executives has revealed, those executives whose careers were derailed by some event had about the same number of such events as those executives who were not derailed. The difference was all in how these people responded to difficult events. Those who were derailed brooded about their problems, didn't talk to others, and made little attempt to rectify the consequences of what had happened. Those who weren't derailed did precisely the opposite. They flew into action, talked to people who would be affected by their mistake, did their best to rectify the problem, and then proceeded to forget about it and move on.[7]

It is clear that the leaders who had greater resilience also had much greater composure in stressful situations. They did not blame others, snap at subordinates, or berate others for some action. Instead, they were poised and gracefully admitted any mistake that they had made.

The positive emotions that we've been discussing have the capacity to essentially erase the consequences of negative events in our lives and create the capacity to be resilient in the face of adversity.

CONCLUSION

We have proposed that leaders inspire and motivate those about them. The outcomes that they want to achieve fall roughly into these two categories:

1. New behaviors and outcomes, especially higher productivity
2. New attitudes and emotions, such as confidence, optimism and hope, initiative, responsibility, enthusiasm, and resilience

The leader is able to do this because all emotions are highly contagious from one individual to the next. This fact is magnified when one person has "role power" in the organization by virtue of having a position of responsibility. The stronger the emotions that are expressed by the leader and the more willing and able the leader is to convey these emotions, the more change occurs within those being led. And the more formal the "boss-subordinate" relationship is, the more the boss's emotions will be infused into the subordinate.

Chapter 4

A Foundation for Understanding Inspiration

There is nothing noble about being superior to some other man. The true nobility is in being superior to your previous self.

—Hindu Proverb

I have missed more than 9,000 shots in my career. I have lost almost 300 games. On 26 occasions I have been entrusted to take the game-winning shot ... and missed. And I have failed over and over and over again in my life. And that is why I succeed.

—Michael Jordan

As we briefly mentioned in Chapter 1, the empirical foundation for this book came from our research for an earlier book, *The Extraordinary Leader*. For that book, we examined the results from more than 200,000 assessments on 20,000 leaders to identify the behaviors that best differentiated extraordinary leaders. These were the most noticeable behaviors. While many other leadership behaviors have been described in the literature, the 16 that we identified tended to be those that were consistently associated with exceptional leadership. The basic notion of this research was that some behaviors counted much more than others, and that if leaders could improve these behaviors, it would make more of a difference. Leaders who improved these behaviors stood a much better chance of being perceived as great leaders. Based on that research, hundreds of organizations around the world started to use these 16 differentiating behaviors as the basis for their competency models. This has enabled us to collect tens of thousands of assessments using a 360-degree feedback instrument that specifically measures these 16 differentiating competencies.

WHICH OF THE 16 BEHAVIORS DIFFERENTIATES THE MOST?

As data on these differentiating behaviors were accumulated over the last several years, we asked the question, "Which of the 16 is the *best* differentiator?" Out of more than 100,000 assessments on almost 8,000 leaders, a clear first among equals emerged. The item identified as the highest-ranking differentiating behavior is *inspires and motivates to high performance.* Specifically, this analysis showed that when comparing the top 10 percent of leaders to the bottom 10 percent, this one behavior most powerfully separated these two groups. We also compared the top 10 percent against the first through the fiftieth percentiles and found the same result.

In our continued analysis of various data sets from different organizations, countries, and cultures, we found that whenever that competency was used, it was invariably the best differentiator.

We performed another analysis with this set of assessment data. In listing each of the 16 differentiating behaviors, we asked raters to choose which differentiating behavior, *if done with a high level of skill,* would have the greatest impact on the leader's ability to be successful in his current job.

Again, the competency that was chosen most frequently was *inspires and motivates to high performance.* The leaders who were being assessed chose that as the one competency with the most impact.

As we coached leaders around the world, we took note of how many selected *inspires and motivates to high performance* as the strength they most wanted to build. This item again was their most frequent choice.

After we discovered these results, we asked a more difficult question regarding the bottom-line impact of this item: "Are there measurable outcomes that inspirational leaders create?"

As we explained in Chapter 2, a unique addition to our standard 360-degree assessments is a measure of employee commitment from the direct reports of each leader. The employee commitment index asks each person who directly reports to the leader to respond to five questions about her personal work experience. These questions assess the following:

- Satisfaction with the organization
- Intention to stay employed
- Willingness to give extra effort
- Confidence in the success of the organization
- The extent to which she would recommend this organization to others as a good place to work

This index has a very strong correlation with other popular employee engagement indexes.

WHAT MAKES A LEADER EXTRAORDINARY?

Our previous research for *The Extraordinary Leader* found that leaders who had exceptional leadership ability (e.g., above the eightieth or ninetieth percentile) were able to achieve substantially better outcomes. Extraordinary leaders had lower turnover, higher customer satisfaction, higher profitability, and higher commitment and engagement on the part of their employees. In Chapter 2 we showed similar results for leaders who were very effective at inspiring and motivating others. All this analysis led to the question, "How do leaders move from being good at inspiring others to being extraordinary?"

When we looked at exceptional leaders, we discovered several things that we had expected, and a few things that surprised us. We were not surprised that they were not perfect, nor were we surprised that the qualities that made them extraordinary were different for different people.

When we asked groups to think about a leader whom they would consider extraordinary, we then asked, "What did that leader do exceptionally well?" "What were that leader's strengths?" In response, we heard a variety of different answers:

- The leader had a clear vision and communicated it effectively.
- The leader drove hard for exceptional results.
- The leader cared about and developed people.
- The leader had high integrity and honesty.
- The leader was technically savvy.

We then asked if the leader had any weaknesses. Nearly everyone, when asked, could readily identify a weakness, even in these extraordinary leaders. Often the weaknesses were not trivial. Some leaders lacked the ability to think strategically, while others had difficulty staying on top of the administrative detail of their position. Some lacked people skills and preferred to "hole up" in their office. Others were novices regarding the technology of the business and resisted "rolling in the dirt" when it came to anything technical.

This exercise demonstrates exactly what we found in our research. What characterized extraordinary leaders was not the absence of weaknesses. Rather, it was the presence of a few profound strengths. All leaders seemed to have some weaknesses, but the real differentiation of a great leader from a poor leader was that extraordinary leaders had profound strengths and used a variety of mechanisms to compensate for any weaknesses. In some cases, that meant hiring someone with complementary skills. In other cases, it meant restructuring the job so that others performed the activities that the executive struggled with. Many people assume that the path to extraordinary performance is to eliminate all weaknesses. Their unspoken assumptions are, "Whatever strengths I have will take care of themselves," and "Getting better means discovering what I'm bad at and fixing that." Therefore, they focus their development efforts on the things they don't do well.

The problem with this approach is that typically people are not very interested in or passionate about their most significant weaknesses, and therefore they don't improve much. We have found that a key to improvement for every person is to have passion.

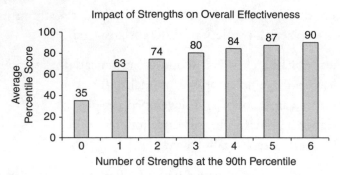

Figure 4-1 Number of Strengths Compared to Perceived Effectiveness

Working on a behavior that you are interested in creates a much higher probability that real change will occur.

The analysis that propelled us to this conclusion was one that specifically looked at the impact of strengths. Strength in a competency was defined as performing at the nineteenth percentile. The results confirmed that it wasn't the absence of flaws but the presence of strengths that made exceptional leaders. We recently conducted a new analysis, using another substantial database, and found extremely similar results. Figure 4-1 comes from the second study and shows the results from 7,195 leaders.

In this study, leaders were assessed on the 16 differentiating competencies. Note in the figure that leaders with no strengths have an average effectiveness rating of the thirty-fifth percentile. But when leaders do one thing very well, their effectiveness rating jumps to the sixty-third percentile. Strength in just 3 out of the 16 lifts people to the eightieth percentile.

HOW DO LEADERS DEVELOP PROFOUND STRENGTHS?

Once we understood the impact of profound strengths, we wanted to understand how leaders go about developing a profound strength. Most people assume that the same process that helps a person move from poor to good performance would work for going from ordinary to extraordinary performance. In our previous book, on how leaders can become extraordinary,[1] we describe our conclusion that the process of building a strength requires a radically different approach from that used to fix a weakness.

The following case study illustrates the problem with this approach:

> When Ralph first joined the company as a new graduate in mechanical engineering, he did not know much about how to build a rocket engine. When asked if his undergraduate schooling had prepared him for this kind of work, he said, "Well, it provided some theoretical insights, but I think that playing with fireworks in the backyard was more helpful."
>
> To learn the fundamentals, Ralph was assigned to work with an engineer who had been building rockets for 20 years. He was an excellent mentor. Ralph also attended technical conferences and started reading journals and technical papers related to this new field. He worked hard to learn all that he could, and after five years his mentor told him that Ralph knew more than he did about building rockets.
>
> Ralph was promoted to manage a new project, but as he began his new assignment, he felt that his technical knowledge was good but not great. He enjoyed the technical aspects of his job and wanted to use his technical and analytical skills as a platform for his career. The difficult question was, "How do I move from good to great?" His mentor could not really help him, and all of his peers were generally at the same technical level. He had read all the literature that was available and felt that he was up-to-date, but no one thought of him as having a profound strength in his technical expertise. Classes, reading, mentoring, and varied assignments had helped Ralph learn the basics and go from being a newbie to possessing a reasonable level of competence. Yet for Ralph to develop a

profound strength in his technical expertise, it was going to require him to do something different from what he had done before. His approach had to change.

THE INTERACTION OF STRENGTHS

Most people assume that individuals can be great in one thing without being exceptionally competent in other areas. In a recent workshop a participant asked the question, "Can a leader be at the ninety-ninth percentile on drive for results and the first percentile on interpersonal skills?" The reply from one of the authors was no. To have an exceptional ability to deliver results, leaders would need to have trust and cooperation from their direct reports. A useful way to visualize this is to think of competencies as having bungee cords connecting them. There is only so much stretch in the bungee cord. When the difference between competencies become extreme, one competency pulls back on the other competency. A careful examination of the data, however, reveals a fascinating pattern. For leaders with one strength at the ninetieth percentile, on average their second-highest-scoring competency was at the eighty-fourth percentile, and their third-highest-scoring competency was at the seventy-ninth percentile. The bottom line is, leaders who scored high on one competency were, in general, remarkably good at a few other competencies. Simply stated, there is an amazing inter-action effect among various competencies. The following analysis demonstrates these interaction effects.

Three competencies were analyzed to understand the power of the interactions between them. We examined those leaders who were at the seventy-fifth percentile or higher on each of the three competencies and found the percentage of leaders who were at the ninetieth percentile in overall leadership effectiveness who possessed only one of the characteristics. Keep in mind that a competency at the seventy-fifth percentile would not be considered a profound strength but rather a competency where a person is moderately good. The three competences are shown in Chart 4-1.

Chart 4-1 Extraordinary Leaders Rarely Have a Single Strength

Technical/Analytical Skills	Drive for Results	People Skills	Percentage of Leaders at the 90th Percentile
Strength above the 75th percentile	Not a strength	Not a strength	0%

Technical/Analytical Skills	Drive for Results	People Skills	Percentage of Leaders at the 90th Percentile
Not a strength	Strength above the 75th percentile	Not a strength	0.5%

Technical/Analytical Skills	Drive for Results	People Skills	Percentage of Leaders at the 90th Percentile
Not a strength	Not a strength	Strength above the 75th percentile	1.4%

This analysis demonstrates that being moderately good at one competency does not guarantee that you will be perceived as extraordinary in an overall way. In fact, the probabilities are so low that you could describe it as almost impossible.

We then looked at leaders who possessed more than one of these three competencies at the seventy-fifth percentile. When leaders possessed combinations of strengths, they were elevated to the highest ranks of leadership in their organizations.

Note the interaction effect when a person is competent at all three skills (see Chart 4-2).

Chart 4-2 The Power of Combining Competencies

Technical/ Analytical Skills	Drive for Results	People Skills	Percentage of Leaders at the 90th Percentile
Strength above the 75th percentile	Strength above the 75th percentile	Strength above the 75th percentile	87%

The results are quite dramatic. As you consider the case involving Ralph and his dilemma on how to improve his technical ability, it might stand to reason that when one improves other skills, one's technical skills might be more fully utilized. For example, Ralph might understand the technical issues but not be very effective at communicating those issues to his team.

After looking at these data and testing these conclusions for more than five years, it has become clear to us that the way leaders develop strengths is by utilizing other skills. It is the combination of skills that creates profound strength. Great dishes prepared by the best chefs are not the result of a single ingredient; they are the result of a recipe with multiple ingredients. Great leadership comes about by mixing the right leadership competencies together and finding the right chemistry to create powerful combinations.

MOVING FROM ORDINARY TO EXTRAORDINARY

How does a leader move from being ordinary to being extraordinary at inspiring others? In Chapter 2 we described the impact of inspiration on a number of critical outcomes. The better leaders were at inspiring others, the better they did on each of the outcomes. In today's organizations, with fierce competition and ever-increasing demands, there is a significant need for leaders who can inspire.

Because good does not equal great when it comes to inspiration, how does a leader make this transition to becoming an extraordinary inspirer of others? Almost everyone knows someone who tries too hard to inspire and motivate others to high performance by simply turning up the volume. There are at least two different approaches.

Positive Approach

This would include the following:

- Pep talks and platitudes

- Catchphrases, such as "You can do it," "Never give up," or "The sky is the limit"
- Extreme optimism that fails to recognize realities

> Jan was very frustrated. She had tried several times to get her manager to understand that there was a significant problem with a project she was working on. "Every time I go to my manager and try to help him understand the problem, he listens for a few minutes and then starts saying things like, "Jan, I know you can do it" or "I am confident that we can overcome any problems if we just try harder."
>
> Jan went on to say, "As I try to explain the problem further, I can tell that, first, he doesn't understand anything that I am talking about, and, second, he just doesn't care." Jan was convinced that her manager merely wanted the problem to go away. Her final comment was, "What drives me nuts is that he thinks that stupid speech motivates me—it does just the opposite."

Negative Approach

- Constant reminders of what people are doing wrong
- Unrelenting nagging
- Pushing people to achieve better results

> Jim was a senior manager in charge of a large group of engineers. He commented that he hated Mondays. He went on to say that every Monday he had a standing 30-minute call with his manager. "I just can't stand her grinding on me every week," he said. He went on to say, "Those 30 minutes of harangue are about all I can take." When asked what grinding was, Jim replied, "It's just continually reminding me of our performance problems, asking me what went wrong, how can I prevent this in the future, why didn't I see that problem coming, and specifically what am I going to do about the problem this week."

When asked if the "grinding" motivated him to improve, Jim commented, "It doesn't matter how well we do or what we accomplish; she'll always find something to grind on me about."

NONLINEAR APPROACH

How, then, can a person become extremely good at a specific skill? To understand this, we looked at evaluations from 183,463 colleagues regarding 14,466 leaders. We found groups of competencies that, when paired with "inspiring and motivating others," created powerful combinations. We called these *competency companions*.

The combination of the two skills—the desired one and a companion one—increases effectiveness and is often easier to carry out. For example, consider how an ice skater might use a combination of skills to increase effectiveness. A great ice skater can jump into the air and land gracefully on the ice. Coordination is certainly a critical skill for the skater. But performing a jump that rises only two inches off the ice is not going to be very thrilling. Add a companion skill, such as strength, and it is another story. A triple axel is very thrilling and requires great strength, but it's thrilling only if the skater doesn't fall while landing the jump. The combination of coordination and strength is what makes the skater effective.

In our research, we looked at people who were highly effective in a specific behavior. Detailed analysis showed that people who were most effective in performing Behavior A also rated highly in several companion behaviors (Behaviors B, C, D, E, and F). Similarly, people who rated poorly in performing Behavior A also rated poorly in the same companion behaviors. It became clear that improving performance in companion behaviors might facilitate improvement in the specific behavior.

For additional information and resources on nonlinear companions, on the importance of strengths, and on the heightened success that comes from developing strengths versus weaknesses, go to www.zengerfolkman.com and click on the Inspiring Leader icon.

Part 2

The Making of an
Inspirational Leader

In this section of the book, we present the necessary attributes of highly inspiring leaders, along with the specific behaviors that they use. Our metaphor is that of a battery pack. We liken the attributes of the leader to the battery pack container. The battery pack, in our metaphor, represents the leader's willingness to do these things:

1. Be a role model and an example for others
2. Push for constant change and improvement
3. Continually take the initiative to make good things happen

Chapter 5 describes the role these attributes play in inspiration.

Chapter 6 leaps into the world of emotion and the powerful role it plays. Emotion can be thought of as the wiring and switch of the battery pack.

Chapters 7 through 12 describe six behaviors that we liken to the batteries that get inserted into the battery pack. The batteries are the following:

1. Setting stretch goals
2. Creating vision and direction
3. Communicating powerfully
4. Developing people
5. Being collaborative and a good team player
6. Fostering innovation

Which batteries get used at any one time doesn't appear to make much difference. There are many useful combinations in which several batteries combine their energy to make excellent things happen. While the six behaviors just noted are in descending order of statistical significance in their linkage to "inspiring and motivating to high performance," the differences are not huge. The choice of which to use depends on which appears to be most needed and the leader's level of comfort in using it.

Chapter 5

Attributes of the Inspirational Leader

A leader leads by example, whether he intends to or not.
—Anonymous

There is nothing more difficult to take into hand, more perilous to conduct or more uncertain in its success, than to take the lead in the introduction of a new order of things.
—Niccolò Machiavelli

As we consider the necessary attributes of a leader who is capable of inspiring, there are a trio of fundamental characteristics that are vital in order to make inspiration come to life. These attributes are the cornerstone of what it takes to inspire and motivate others.

1. Role model
2. Change champion
3. Initiator

Before we dive into what these attributes mean and why they have such an impact, it is worth noting why we have separated them from the remaining characteristics. The reason? They are broad attributes or qualities, not specific behaviors that the leader practices. They create the foundation for all of the other attributes that are important in motivating and inspiring others. In short, these attributes have a pervasive quality that makes them stand apart because they play into so many different areas of leadership and are not defined by a singular area of competence.

Because they are broad, they do not simply represent something that you go and do. And that is another reason that these three are set apart from the rest. They represent a pattern of actions that form other people's impression of who you are. Additionally, as we analyzed the written comments contained in the 360-degree assessments on tens of thousands of leaders and began to group them into categories, a pattern began to emerge that pointed to these three attributes being the broad attributes that separate those who inspire and those who do not.

We've discovered that if you ask people what behavior on the part of a leader inspires them, it is not an easy question to answer. Yet if you press someone to answer this question, the answers will often fall into one of these three categories. So what are they? Are they roles? Are they functions? Are they patterns of behavior? Are they the glue that holds other behaviors together? Or are they the medium in which other behaviors grow? Whatever they are, we do know this for certain: they are highly correlated with inspiration, and we could not ignore them.

We'll call them attributes, and in this chapter we'll explore what they mean in practical terms, examine why they may be so highly correlated with inspiration, and provide some practical suggestions for how people can get better at them.

Sometimes a metaphor or model helps us to both understand and remember such a concept. As we noted earlier in the book, there are many factors that contribute to a leader's excelling, yet it seems clear that inspiration is what gives leadership its energy. That energy is stored and channeled, and it fuels inspiration. In this spirit, we submit the metaphor of a battery pack that is designed to power any device that requires an energy source— possibly a camera or a flashlight. This battery pack holds several individual batteries. It aligns the batteries' polarity, connects them, and enables them to deliver their power to the device. The three attributes listed earlier in this chapter are akin to the battery pack container, into which are inserted several batteries. The battery pack, in our metaphor, represents the leader's willingness to be a role model and example for others, to push for constant change and improvement, and finally to continually take the initiative to make good things happen.

The use of emotions becomes the "on–off" switch on the battery pack. The attributes we have described are the container for specific leadership behaviors leaders can use. The leader now inserts one or more of six batteries (behaviors) into the overall battery pack. The more power the battery pack can produce, the more the leader is able to inspire and motivate.

The batteries are:

1. Setting stretch goals
2. Creating vision and direction
3. Communicating powerfully
4. Developing people
5. Being collaborative and a good team player
6. Fostering innovation

Which batteries get used at any one time doesn't make much difference, although our research indicates that having more battery power creates greater energy for inspiration. There are many useful combinations in which several batteries combine their energy to make good things happen. While the six behaviors just noted are in descending order of statistical significance in their linkage to "inspiring and motivating to high performance," the statistical variances of their impact are not huge. The choice of which to use depends on which appears to be most needed and the leader's level of comfort in using it. What's more, the amount to which these batteries can be used seems to have no limit (in fact, more use often supports more use), so they provide an energy source for leadership that is renewable. First, on to the battery pack—the container for this renewable source of leadership energy.

ROLE MODEL

How do people learn how to behave? How does a child learn the acceptable ways to eat a meal? To interact on the playground? To get dressed in the morning? Or how does a newly hired intern learn how to behave in a corporate meeting? Or how does a new manager learn about the culture of the organization she is joining?

The most powerful and useful explanation has been labeled "social learning theory" or "behavior modeling." The point is simply that we learn the most by watching what others do and then imitating that behavior. While that may happen with greatest frequency in our growing-up years, it continues through life.

What Our Research Showed

The most effective leaders were excellent role models. Simply put, they exemplified what the organization stood for and how it wanted people to behave. Indeed, some have theorized that the people chosen for leadership roles are those who best epitomize the characteristics that are most valued by the organization. They are sensitive to the fact that how they behave will be watched by others, and that this, in turn, will directly shape the behavior of their subordinates. These individuals were willing to discipline their own behavior so that they became excellent examples of what the organization stands for, believes in, and rewards.

Much has been said about why people leave organizations. The cliché has emerged that people don't quit the company, they quit their boss. Our research confirms that the boss has an enormous impact on how people behave and whether they stay or leave the organization. In addition, the example the boss sets has a tremendous impact on the level of enthusiasm and motivation of the entire work group.

Ponder for a moment how far-reaching the leader's example becomes. By simple deeds and words, enormously important messages are conveyed. For example, the boss's

- Pace sets the rhythm for the entire organization
- Working hours become the accepted pattern of work
- Use of company resources sets the acceptable standard
- Interaction with team members and others establishes a cultural norm

- Use of alcohol at company functions sets the accepted practice
- Focus on specific issues or opportunities becomes the focus of the organization
- Willingness to own up to mistakes sets the pattern for the entire organization's willingness to be accountable

In short, there is no limit to the far-reaching impact of the leader's example on the overall behavior of the organization.

To demonstrate the impact of being a positive role model, we examined ratings from 34,098 employees. The employees rated the effectiveness of their immediate manager at being a role model. We then analyzed the level of employee commitment for each of those employees. Figure 5-1 shows the results.

As the study demonstrates, employees who felt that their manager needed significant improvement in being a role model responded only 41 percent positively on the commitment index, while those who felt that their leader was a positive role model and had a significant strength in that area responded 88 percent positively to the commitment index. There is a substantial negative impact when

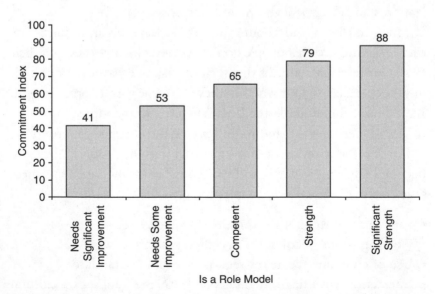

Figure 5-1 Impact of Being a Role Model on Employee Commitment

leaders fail to walk their talk and a positive impact for those who act as role models.

Do as I Say, Not as I Do

Consider the negative impact of a "do as I say, not as I do" kind of leader. What kind of effect does this leader have on the team that he is responsible for? In most cases, people eventually grow tired of the double standards these leaders live by and cease to be willing to give all they can for such leaders. Our research on this topic indicated that there is a stark difference between the results achieved by leaders who are great role models for the company and exemplify the behaviors that are of greatest value to the organization and those achieved by leaders who are not. When we study employee engagement, it is clear that those leaders who received high rankings in the areas of "Can always be counted on to follow through on commitments" and "Works hard to 'walk the talk' and avoids saying one thing and doing another" were able to drive significantly higher levels of engagement and commitment from those who they led.

These data sets illustrate just how powerful the impact of a great role model is on two important indexes. In terms of both employee retention and creating an environment that drives maximum productivity, role modeling is one of the essentials for leaders to inspire and motivate. There are several reasons why that is.

Role Models Cause Organizational Behaviors to Proliferate

Have you ever worked with certain people and thought to yourself, "I'd like to be like them"? Perhaps you felt this way not about every aspect of these people's lives, but about traits that you admired or saw as beneficial or desirable. Most of us have had this experience, whether the people involved were our managers, other leaders, peers, or even those outside of work. When someone is an effective role model, it inspires people to behave in a way consistent with the way that person leads or behaves and has a powerful implication; role models of traits or behaviors cause those traits to proliferate within organizations.

In our earlier research for *The Extraordinary Leader,* which identified the 16 competencies that differentiated the best and the worst leaders, one of the competencies that emerged as a critical strength from which all others flowed was character. While a thorough discussion of character is outside the scope of this book, displaying strong character is closely aligned with being a compelling role model who propels people to greater levels of achievement. Leaders inspire others by doing what they say they will do, demonstrating conviction in a course of action, and exemplifying the behaviors that they want emulated with a "do as I do" approach.

Another reason this becomes so vital is that people who are led by a good role model are willing to put forth incredible amounts of effort. One of the reasons for this extra effort or intensified commitment is often that people do not want to let the leader down. When leaders are able to instill this feeling in the people whom they are responsible for, there are typically much higher levels of productivity and commitment.

> In his first job, one of the authors worked for a small not-for-profit organization. The executive director of the organization had created a terrific culture that was rigorously focused on performance. The people in the organization would routinely work evenings and weekends, not only out of commitment to the organization's cause, but because they so respected the leader that they would do anything in their power not to let him down. The executive director was a classic role model of the type of leader the young staff members wanted to emulate, and as a result, he was able to drive high levels of performance.

One of the statements we ask people to rate in our 360-degree feedback instruments is, "My work environment is a place where people want to go the extra mile," and the results are constant in each of the hundreds of data sets we review each year. The highest levels of commitment go hand in hand with leaders who perform at the highest levels of being an effective role model and setting a good example. This is an indisputable driver of employee engagement and organizational performance.

How Leaders Can Become Better Role Models

1. *Lead through example.* The first step in becoming an outstanding role model is deciding that you will see that your personal behavior conforms to everything you want other people to do. As we mentioned earlier, some leaders believe it is possible to have a double standard that says, "Do what I say, but pay no attention to what I do." But that seldom works. People invariably pay most attention to what the leader does, and their behavior moves in that direction.

   The essence of being a sound role model is simple. The leader basically communicates, "Do anything you see me doing." This standard puts pressure on the leader. Every day in every way, the leader is serving as an example for others to follow. This represents a major commitment. But the reality is that others in the organization will follow the leader's example, regardless of the decision that the leader makes. Inspiration and motivation come when the leader's behavior is in complete alignment with what the organization espouses.

2. *Maximize exposure.* If a leader is a good role model, and if the leader's behavior is consistent with the organization's values, there is great benefit to increasing the exposure of the people in the organization to the leader.

   What are some of the ways to increase that exposure?

   - *"All hands" meetings.* These meetings provide the opportunity for everyone to interact with the leader. Such meetings have the potential to inspire and motivate large numbers of employees as they hear important messages firsthand from the leader.

- *MBWA.* Management by walking around was a popular idea in the 1990s that isn't talked about much in today's world. But the idea of the leader's getting out of the office and connecting with people at their workplace is still a powerful, useful idea. Many important messages are conveyed by the simple act of the leader's taking the time to drop by and show interest in others.
- *Visits to remote locations.* In today's organizations, the workforce is seldom under one roof, or even on the same campus. Increasingly there are satellite offices, small research teams scattered around the globe, and highly dispersed manufacturing or service groups. People who work there often feel isolated from the parent organization. Visits from senior leaders have a strongly motivational impact, depending on the leader's nature and behavior.
- *Recounting stories.* How is a strong culture created and disseminated inside an organization? Alan Wilkins, while conducting research at Stanford University, determined that it was stories told by the leaders that created and shaped culture.[1]

  One of the hallmarks of HP's culture was informality that they believed helped to increase communication between levels of the organization. An oft repeated story has David Packard meeting a new employee who addresses him as "Mr. Packard." Seemingly without hesitation, Packard said to the employee, "My father is often referred to as Mr. Packard, but I'd prefer that you call me 'Dave.'" That story, with some variations, was used to drive home the point about the importance of informality at HP.

3. *Selectively model behaviors that need to be emphasized in the organization.* Many leaders lament the lack of accountability that exists in their organization. People fail to own up to the mistakes that they make and to readily acknowledge their personal role in some of the things that go wrong inside a department.

4. *Seek feedback regarding inconsistencies between a leader's behavior and the espoused values of the organization.* The highest expression of a leader's taking the position of role model seriously is the leader's eagerness to ensure that there are no disconnects between the important signals the leader wants to send and how people are interpreting the leader's daily behavior.

> One great value from leaders obtaining 360-degree feedback from peers, direct reports, and their boss is that they become aware of those places where the disconnect comes as a surprise to them. A bank executive with whom we work is a prime example of an executive who doesn't just accept feedback, but willingly seeks it out because he sees the huge payoffs it produces. He went so far as to have his wife complete the 360-degree process for him, because she attended many company functions with him and he thought her perspective would be valuable. While many executives seek to shrink the number and variety of people providing feedback to them, he went in exactly the opposite direction.

CHANGE CHAMPION

It has been well chronicled that one of the main contrasts between leadership and management is the leader's role in implementing change. If a leader is going to truly inspire others, then the ability to motivate a change of some kind is a key ingredient. Not much inspiration or motivation is needed to maintain the status quo or simply plod along. All progress demands change, yet we know that if people are uncertain about the impact of a change on them personally, there is a high likelihood that some of them will resist the change. And it goes without saying that if people perceive the change as having a detrimental effect on them, they will most certainly resist it. So the leader who is responsible for new directions and strategy, growth, adapting to competition, or any other shift must be able to propel and sustain change effectively.

Of course, change always has its resistance and skeptics, and there are often more than leaders think. The prevailing attitudes toward many changes in organizations today, be they explicit or implied, is captured in the popular 1990s *Saturday Night Live* sketch "Lothar of the Hill People," where comedian Mike Myers comments on a change proposed by a fellow tribesman, "It is a good idea, but it is a new idea, and since it is new we fear it, and since we fear it we must reject it." These common attitudes about change require a leader to develop strength in leading change if she is to be successful in moving any operation forward.

There are many models for change, and next to leadership, there are few topics that have been more written about in the last decade. Regardless of the model for change du jour, there are several competencies that a leader must display if she is to inspire and motivate others to produce a positive, intentional change.

It is worth noting that not every change effort will necessarily require a leader to be a champion of change. A change in strategic direction or a central process improvement is a far different effort from a change that affects a simple administrative policy. Some changes simply need to be clarified and enforced. For our purposes of exploring how the best leaders drive change, we are specifically considering issues that are of significance.

When we examined and analyzed those leaders who were profoundly strong in the area of creating and driving change, we saw a unique ability to energize others whom they worked with and to rally support for a cause that was uncommon in their peer group. Those leaders' ability to create compelling cases for change and to communicate to others how a change would positively affect them were some of the obvious differentiators of success. In our research, we were able to isolate the factors that were at the intersection for those leaders who were exceptionally inspiring and able to produce change. In doing this, we were able to easily see how affecting change had such a significant impact on the ability of a leader to inspire.

1. *Persuasion is at the heart of the matter.* One of the key behaviors needed for a leader to be an effective champion of change is the

ability to persuade. This is not based on pushing, cajoling, or even begging (though some less effective leaders rely on these tactics to persuade). Rather, it is based on the leader's ability to relate to others and understand what fears or doubts people have regarding a specific change. Leaders must be able to understand those fears and articulate an intended change in such a way that the majority of the people affected will be convinced of the need for change. There is a commonly held belief that in order to do this well, a leader must create a sense of urgency. While this may in fact be true in some cases, leaders have to be careful with this.

> One of the authors worked with a senior executive who had read a book on change management and decided that for every change implemented in the company, the first step was that urgency had to be created. In every change effort, the first part of the implementation was to create urgency about the change. The first three or four times it worked. After that, the urgency was viewed as theatrics, and by the time the company was working to create urgency around even the simplest of changes, it became trite and ineffective.

Most of the time leaders persuade by providing clarity on the topics of (1) why this change, (2) why now, and (3) why in this manner. This, coupled with your conviction and the other key behaviors leaders use to drive change, will be plenty persuasive.

2. *It's the results of the change that matter.* Of the hundreds of organizations we work with each year, we never see any of them invest in a change effort, whether it is a new strategy, a process improvement, or the launch of an initiative, because it is fun or because they just feel that they should. There is most frequently a clear line of sight between the change that is being undertaken and a clear desired end result that the organization will achieve by making this shift. Having an outcomes orientation helps a change champion maintain a balanced focus on the results being

achieved and on how the organization is making the change. As much as we try to avoid overreferencing sports on the topics of motivation and inspiration, there is an apropos saying among coaches, "Nothing brings a team together like winning." Driving for and achieving results together is motivating and inspiring for all who are active participants, and this is particularly true when undertaking a major challenge, which many change efforts are. Inspirational leaders provide energy and passion about the achievement of goals and milestones, which instills pride and commitment in people. This builds on itself over time and becomes part of a culture of achievement that the leader can create, with an eye on the results of any change effort.

3. *Recognize those who made it happen and they will do it again.* As we discuss the results achieved through a change effort, it is worth noting that we are not simply talking about the final outcomes achieved. In some cases, that may take years. Leaders who are powerful champions of change are able to recognize the key milestones along the path of any change effort and take a moment to pause and recognize those who made the change happen. This is vital because a tremendous part of making a change effort work through other people and inspiring them to sustain performance is making sure that they know—and that the entire organization knows—the value of their contribution. This recognition, be it verbal, written, monetary, or some other type of acknowledgment, not only begins to cement the importance of new approaches and success, but reinforces the actions or outcomes that an organization seeks. And, of course, that is the first step in replicating success and driving a change effort to fruition.

INITIATOR

If leadership has a hallmark, it is in the role of the initiator. Right or wrong, well executed or not, with or without an effectively managed team, nothing says *leader* like being the initiator. The energy and driving force behind any movement requires a catalyst, and in the role of initiator, a leader has the responsibility to "get the ball rolling." This important element of leadership is at the core of what it means to be an extraordinary leader. The best leaders are those who become the cause (even subtly) of a direction or event. They do not wait for others to choose a path, or allow inaction to make a choice for them. Invariably, one of the responsibilities of a leader is to look beyond the horizon to see issues and opportunities emerging and anticipate the appropriate actions. Taking the initiative and doing something is what unlocks the power of that strategic perspective. These are the leaders who get out in front and make things happen. In our research on extraordinary leaders, when we examined the typical characteristics of leaders who were in the bottom 10 percent or who possessed what we termed a "fatal flaw," the main issues surrounding them were related to the theme of not taking enough initiative.

As we have described earlier about the ways in which inspired colleagues behave, one of those characteristics was that they take the initiative because they do not think of themselves as hired hands, but rather as owners of the business. That behavior, of course, does not just happen—it is modeled and inspired by a leader who is mindful about being the initiator and creating an environment in which taking the initiative is part of the culture and rewarded. The leader as initiator assumes responsibility and is intentional about the decisions that are made and the directions that are chosen.

It Takes More Energy to Start

Sir Isaac Newton studied the movement of objects and formulated his conclusions into laws. The first one was: an object that is at rest will not move until a net force acts upon it.

We're all familiar with the principle and reality of inertia. We've learned that if we have a cup that is full to the brim with any liquid, we're likely to spill it when we start moving. The water wants to stay where it was. We're also prone to spill it when we stop moving or if we change the direction in which we're moving. The liquid wants to keep moving in the same direction and at the same pace that it had been moving. We've also learned that it takes a lot more energy to get something that has been standing still to start to move. While Newton discovered the formula to describe that, we've all had practical experience that teaches us that reality.

In many high-efficiency hybrid vehicles, there is a display that shows the miles per gallon based on the current speed of the vehicle. A quick observation of this display reveals that in going from a dead stop to 35 miles per hour, the miles per gallon gauge settles in at around 25 miles per gallon. Once the vehicle is traveling at 35 miles per hour, however, the miles per gallon gauge quickly adjusts to 50 miles per gallon. It becomes obvious that the amount of energy required to get an object moving is greater than the amount of energy required to keep that object moving. This same principle seems to apply to humans taking the initiative. It takes a lot of energy to get things started. Everyone knows that it is much easier to coast than to start. In order for people to take the initiative, they need to have enough energy in terms of both time and motivation to take on something new, and they need to be willing to expend that energy. Leaders who take the initiative believe that they are responsible for getting things started.

When individuals take the initiative, they may be punished for stepping outside of standard practices. Organizations often reward following rather than taking a different path. Many people who take the initiative and fail learn the lesson that it is often better to sit back, go with the flow, and let other people volunteer.

Why Taking the Initiative Is So Inspiring

After looking at data showing the correlation between employee commitment and leadership behaviors, it has become very clear that what creates satisfaction for people at work is accomplishing challenging assignments and doing significant work. People want to make a difference. They want to accomplish something significant. A key capability in taking on challenging assignments is taking the initiative.

Examining data about the events that are the most frustrating to employees, we see a group of comments that have a common theme. Sample comments focus on work being stalled, waiting for decisions to be made, bureaucratic processes that add no value, and starting projects that get canceled. Delays, cancellations, and needless bureaucracy will make any work environment unmotivating. The one leadership skill that can be the key to solving these kinds of organizational problems is taking the initiative. Leaders who work in organizations that have these kinds of problems sometimes feel that the best thing they can do to help people is to teach them how to cope because the organization cannot be changed. They point to initiatives in the past that have failed. One leader described it this way, "This company is like a one million pound marshmallow. If you dropped an atom bomb in it, the bomb would be swallowed up and absorbed. Perhaps the marshmallow would shake a little, but nothing would fundamentally change." Leaders who take the initiative are willing to try. They continue to make efforts to improve. They feel that they are accountable for making something happen, and this is inspiring to other people.

Of the three attributes in this chapter, taking the initiative is sometimes one of the hardest things to do. Typically there are a variety of things that get in the way or block people from taking the initiative. Let's look at why.

Feeling Overwhelmed Gets in the Way of Initiative

If you feel totally and completely overwhelmed, then you are not very likely to volunteer for a new assignment or find some additional piece of work that has not been done. That feeling of barely keeping your head above water or juggling 20 balls makes you worry that taking on one additional item will cause you to drown or to drop all the balls. In today's organizations, almost everyone feels overwhelmed. Almost everyone has more to do than can be done. This is one of the side effects of flattening and downsizing organizations. While everyone is busy, there are still a few leaders who continue to take the initiative. What, then, is the difference between those who continue to take the initiative and those who feel overwhelmed?

First, feeling overwhelmed is partly an emotion (the extent to which you feel oppressed) and partly reality (the number of things you need to accomplish). Those who feel oppressed believe that the solution to being overwhelmed is to reduce the number of responsibilities or items on the to-do list. Often the problem is more about the feelings that people experience than about the size of the list. The lists will never go away, but when people feel that they are victims with no control, this will negatively affect their behavior. In a study of new mothers, researchers found that the frustration of constant child care often resulted in their stopping their planning and organization. Whenever they made a plan, the immediate needs of a new baby would often force them to cancel or reschedule that plan. After repeated experiences, many new mothers simply gave up and quit planning. If a person can change her attitude from being oppressed to being empowered, then initiative can begin.

Second, having clear priorities is critical. On every person's list there are a few critical priorities and a large number of other issues. Leaders need to feed the critical priorities and starve or delegate the others.

Third, no one is perfect, so accomplish what you can and move on. Many people believe that they will be judged by what they don't accomplish rather than by what they do accomplish. If you are focused on the high-priority issues and accomplish them well, that is what people will remember.

Fourth, always look for a better way. Innovation can solve many problems and improve productivity, but it also takes some initiative to be more innovative.

Fifth, the problem can be a lack of confidence. Without confidence, people tend to do only what is expected and needed. They resist taking on any additional work or volunteering for assignments. They have a tendency to sit back and let other people offer suggestions and take on difficult assignments. Leaders who lack confidence have a strong fear of failure. There are many ways in which a leader can take the initiative, but those who lack confidence get into the habit of sitting back and letting others take the lead.

How to Take More Initiative

Three factors that become preeminent when we look at the profiles of leaders who are great initiators are decisiveness, accountability, and understanding risk.

Decisiveness
This is not simply a go-for-it mentality—boiling decisiveness down to that glib statement doesn't do the initiator justice. Having a bias toward taking quick action is unquestionably a characteristic of initiators, since the success of many efforts depends on their being accomplished in a short time frame. However, decisiveness in the context of inspiring others goes much deeper. Leaders who are decisive about the directions they are initiating have clearly applied thoughtful strategy to the path they are advocating.

As we said, this is not just about picking a direction and going; there must be careful thought applied to the decision based on the leader's desired outcome and knowledge of the situation. In our research, we gathered various leaders from several industries and gave them a case study concerning a major initiative. They were asked to predict the outcomes of the initiative, including any negative consequences. It was instructive to see how accurate they were in forecasting these events. The group in the case study that was responsible for the initiative had not taken the time, nor did it have the discipline, to anticipate the consequences. Chances are, had the people involved taken the time and fostered that discipline, they might have foreseen many of the problems that arose, and the outcomes of the initiative would have been far better.

Planning, organization, and strategic thought combined with an orientation toward action are essential to the leader who needs to be decisive.

There is a very strong correlation between acting quickly and being seen as taking the initiative. Think about a leader who takes a great deal of time to make a simple decision and whose slow pace frustrates everyone. Even though a decision required some initiative, the leader's slow pace gave everyone the impression that they were resisting the decision. When leaders can move quickly, others see that as taking more initiative. Many decisions are not simple and require study, analysis, and discussion. When a leader continually communicates the progress of the decision and is seen by others as moving forward quickly, then people will judge this as taking the initiative. The leader who studies, analyzes, and discusses but never communicates his progress is often viewed as stalling or delaying.

Decisiveness happens not only in the moment that the decision is made, but in the many moments leading up to a decision in which a leader is gathering data and determining what actions are most appropriate. Doing this well facilitates good decisions as well as faster decisions with a clear sense of resolute action.

The philosopher Goethe made a statement about decisiveness that is worth repeating:

> But when I said that nothing had been done I erred in one important matter. We had definitely committed ourselves and were halfway out of our ruts. We had put down our passage money—booked a sailing to Bombay. This may sound too simple, but is great in consequence. Until one is committed, there is hesitancy, the chance to draw back, always ineffectiveness. Concerning all acts of initiative (and creation), there is one elementary truth the ignorance of which kills countless ideas and splendid plans: that the moment one definitely commits oneself, the providence moves too. A whole stream of events

issues from the decision, raising in one's favor all manner of unforeseen incidents, meetings and material assistance, which no man could have dreamt would have come his way.

Accountability

Being brave enough to be accountable for your actions is a rare quality. A large organization suffered a significant loss. The company CEO made a public statement and apologized for the loss. The divisional senior manager sent out an e-mail acknowledging the loss and that it was in his organization, and apologizing for having a negative impact on the performance of the company. The manager of the function where the loss occurred made no public statement or apology. In discussions with her peers, the manager blamed the economy, poor collaboration within the organization, and an inept supervisor but never publicly acknowledged her accountability for her actions or the problems. The reactions of other people to the functional manager were extremely negative. She was trying so hard to avoid accountability and protect her image that it had just the opposite effect.

The opposite of accountability is finger-pointing. When people try to avoid being accountable, they typically look for someone or something else to blame for their mistakes. When this becomes prevalent in an organization, the culture becomes very dysfunctional, with everyone pointing fingers at everyone else when problems arise. When leaders set the example of being accountable, it encourages others to be more accountable.

Risk

For nearly anything to be accomplished, some level of risk must be accepted. Certainly, there is always a probability that events will not turn out exactly as we expect them to. Sometimes the risk is great and at other times it is insignificant, and part of understanding risk is being able to anticipate the consequences of choices. The term *calculated risk* effectively captures the essence of understanding the potential for gains or consequences and making decisions based on commensurate levels of risk.

Some leaders are more risk-averse than others for a variety of reasons, and without placing a value judgment on taking risks great or small, the best leaders in the world always have to manage some level of risk in their business.

Occasionally decisions like the proverbial "bet the company on a new product" or "all or nothing" scenarios present themselves, and this is the stuff that hero or failure stories are made of. Yet most of the time, leaders are in a constant state of evaluating the risks of investments, reorganizations, strategies, and the like in order to make effective decisions for the organization. That said, what do you think inspires people to action and gets them excited about giving their all to a cause—taking some risk or playing it safe? We would submit that, based on our studies of employee engagement and the people's desire to achieve stretch goals, the answer, while not foolish levels of risk, is absolutely not playing it safe. For this reason, understanding and taking calculated and appropriate risks in order to achieve the results desired is a critical part of inspiring others.

A quotation attributed to Abraham Lincoln states, "Tis better to be silent and be thought a fool, than to speak and remove all doubt." This quotation captures many of the fears that leaders have about taking the initiative and the inherent risk involved. Many people believe that doing nothing does not hurt you that much, but taking risks and failing can permanently damage your career. Taking the initiative usually involves some risk. Those who take the initiative stand out. It is true that some organizations have little tolerance for failure. Many people who are afraid of failure get into a mode of avoiding all potential risk rather than carefully choosing those risk opportunities where the rewards are high and the potential for failure is low. Those who are effective at taking risks often set up clear expectations with others before they take on difficult assignments. For example, they spend the time to let everyone know the potential risks, they help managers know the probability of success, and they look for ways to mitigate negative side effects. When everyone has the appropriate expectations, then failure does not look that bad and success looks incredible.

CONCLUSION

When we explore the three attributes of inspirational leaders and understand the interplay of these characteristics, it is easy to understand why they have such a powerful impact. Even without all the data, the intuitive among us can clearly sense these traits in the leaders who have made us want to do more, who have inspired us to great achievement, and whom we did not want to let down. As a role model who embodies those things that are important for everyone to emulate, a change champion who clears the way for a new path to be taken, and an initiator who provides the catalyst for all of this to happen, leaders who inspire possess a unique and powerful combination of these attributes. These attributes become the container that holds the batteries that are described in the following chapters.

We have provided additional resources on our Web site www.zengerfolkman.com (click on the Inspiring Leader icon) to help leaders further develop these broad characteristics that are essential to inspiration.

STEPS TO TAKE

1. Assess your own level of totally accepting the role of leader. Do you accept the fact that 24/7 you are the role model for the people who report to you? Ask some subordinates for any examples of how your behavior might be seen as being contradictory to the espoused values of the organization.

2. To what degree are you seen as the champion of change? Think of examples in the last two weeks where you have been the instigator of change. Have there been any examples of you throwing cold water on a change that was proposed? If you can't think of several examples, then take a few minutes to think about what

changes would have the most positive impact on your organization's performance. Take the lead in making those changes happen.

3. What new programs, projects, or processes have your fingerprints on them? In other words, what have you truly initiated in the last few months? If you can't think of many things, then think hard about what you could initiate that would be of value and would move the organization forward.

4. Deliberately maximize your exposure. Find ways to have more interaction with your subordinates. Hold "all hands" meetings where everyone has a chance to interact with you. Practice management by walking around. Visit remote locations.

5. Reflect on recent changes that have occurred in your work group and who it was that precipitated each change. In a staff meeting or other public forum, give these people sincere recognition for their role in making the changes occur.

6. What changes have been talked about for the past few months in your team? Most groups have some proposals that have been kicking around for months, and they happen when the leader pushes for a decision to be made. What would those be for your group? How could you push the group to some decision?

Chapter 6

Using Emotion: The DNA of Inspiration

Charisma is the mingling of the inner selves of the leader and the followers.

—Charles Lundholm, Harvard anthropologist

An army of sheep led by a lion would defeat an army of lions led by a sheep.

—Arab Proverb

The spirited horse which will try to win the race of its own accord will run even faster if encouraged.

—Ovid

No matter how tough-minded you are, there comes a time when you must acknowledge the role of emotion in people's work life. Jack and Suzy Welch wrote, "Real leaders touch people. They get in their skin, filling their hearts with inspiration, courage and hope. They share the pain at times of loss and are there to celebrate the wins."[1]

There is no escaping the fact that how people feel about their work and their employer plays an enormous role in the success of their work. So what can we conclude about human emotions and their relationship to how leaders inspire?

EMOTIONS AND INSPIRATION: TWO SIDES OF THE SAME COIN

The entire topic of a leader's ability to inspire subordinates comes down to the leader's willingness and ability to both be aware of and comfortably use emotion. One broad and extremely important kind of emotion is enthusiasm. We think of enthusiasm as describing a feeling of excitement, anticipation, and elation about some prospect for the future.

In short, if you want to be more inspirational, understand that you have to become more comfortable in the world of emotions, feelings, and moods. This may sound like a formidable task. You may also be thinking to yourself, "I am what I am," "I'm too old to change," or "I don't want to get into all this squishy emotion stuff."

> To those who would use that excuse, we raise the example of the late Andy Pearson. It happens that Pearson was no spring chicken; in fact, he was in his mid-eighties. But first, a bit of history. Pearson ran PepsiCo for more than 15 years, during which time sales rose from $1 to $8 billion. He also was a McKinsey & Co. managing director and later a Harvard Business School professor. But Pearson was best known for being a tough boss. His picture was on the cover of *Fortune* in 1980 as one of America's 10 toughest bosses. His reputation was built on a brutally abrasive style that featured belittling people, invoking fear, skewering people with his command of numbers, and relentlessly demanding more from people.
>
> Then, when Pearson was in his mid-seventies, he was invited by David Novak, CEO of the combination of Taco Bell, Pizza Hut, and Kentucky Fried Chicken, to become the chairman of the firm. From Novak, Andy Pearson learned an entirely new way to lead. *Fast Company* magazine described his evolution in these terms:
>
> > These days Pearson is focused on a different, more positive emotional agenda: "You say to yourself, If I could only unleash the power of everybody in the organization, instead of just a few people, what could

we accomplish? We'd be a much better company.... Almost overnight, Pearson saw how the human heart drives a company's success—one person at a time— and how this kind of success can't be imposed from the top but must be kindled through attention, awareness, recognition, and reward.

In summing up what then Tricon (now YUM) Corporation had accomplished, David Dorsey, the author of the article about Pearson, wrote:

> Novak has established a culture that elevates the common worker in a way that brings out the emotional drive and commitment that is at the heart of good work. As a result, Pearson has seen employees weep with gratitude in reaction to nothing more than a few simple words of praise. Where before he might have dismissed that kind of display as sentimentality, he now recognizes emotion for what it is: the secret to a company's competitive edge.[2]

Pearson's own conclusion is telling. "The work environment here is the best I've ever seen.... My experience (here) represents the capstone of my career."

> Ultimately it's all about having more genuine concern for the other person. There's a big difference between being tough and being tough minded. There's an important aspect that has to do with humility.[3]

We find particularly telling the comment that emotion is the secret to a company's competitive edge.

EMOTIONS ARE HIGHLY CONTAGIOUS

Think of the most contagious disease you know about. *E. coli*? The common cold? Flu? Medical researchers observe that one sneeze in a room carries nearly a yard and sends millions of germs into the air, traveling at more than 100 miles an hour.

In a similar way, strong emotions within one person get transmitted to others, except that distance is no barrier. We've all been in a meeting where a gloomy, bad-tempered sourpuss manages to cast a pall over the entire session. Such a person has been described as "sucking on a pickle." Without fail, one critical, nit-picking individual can single-handedly change the climate of the meeting.

On the other hand, another person with an upbeat attitude and an infectious laugh also wields a huge amount of influence. The research is clear that when leaders exert themselves, the effect is amplified, largely because of their role.[4] When leaders express strong emotions, this usually arouses similar feelings within those they lead. The leader's emotions are "super contagious."[5] When leaders make positive comments in group meetings, the self-confidence of the individuals in the group is enhanced. They proceed to display higher levels of motivation and set increasingly higher goals.[6] This leader's behavior effectively induces a higher level of trust within everyone in the meeting. This increasing trust level can be measured.[7]

TUNE IN TO YOUR OWN EMOTIONS

We all have good days and bad days. Nearly everyone who has worked inside organizations for a few years can recall someone coming to the boss's assistant to ask, "What kind of mood is the boss in today?" The mood swings of many bosses are extremely wide and carefully monitored.

We hope you personally have lots more good days than bad ones. But it isn't unusual to become aware that you are a bit irritated about something or someone and that this irritation shows through to others. (We're not encouraging that, mind you, but we're realists.) The message to the would-be inspirational leader is quite obvious. If you're having a bad day, limit your interactions with those about you. As much as you can, guard against expressing negative feelings in your interactions with others. If possible, wait until you are in a better mood before setting up any optional meetings, conferences, or phone calls. There are additional resources for how inspiring leaders can utilize emotion to harness the energy of their team. For more information go to www.zengerfolkman.com and click on the Inspiring Leader icon.

> A pilot was on the way to the plane and was encountered by several colleagues who proceeded to badger him about his lack of support for a recent activity that had been initiated by the pilot's union. At the end of this confrontation the pilot notified operations that he was not fit to fly the plane and the flight was cancelled. Passengers were obviously perturbed about this turn of events. But this pilot was aware that his emotional state prevented him from being focused on flying in a totally safe manner, and that delegating the task to the copilot would not provide the fail-safe system of having two competent pilots on board in case of an emergency.
>
> This is an interesting lesson to leaders in businesses who probably should, on some occasions, disqualify themselves from being in command, based on their emotional state.

Conversely, expand your interactions on those days when you're feeling especially positive and enthusiastic. Reach out to more people. Pepper your conversation with positive expressions that will elevate the mood of those about you.

If you are by nature on the pessimistic side of the ledger, we encourage you to investigate the remarkable work on optimism being done by Martin Seligman. His book *Learned Optimism* is an extremely useful treatise that presents compelling evidence of why you should work to become more optimistic (health, career success, marital success, and daily happiness all hinge on it). Better yet, the book gives you practical exercises to help you get there.

BE ATTUNED TO THE EMOTIONS OF THOSE ABOUT YOU

We're all admonished to be better listeners. Good listening can be thought of as moving up a short flight of stairs, with each step being a higher level of listening skill.

- Good listening begins with not talking in order to allow the other party to speak.
- The next step is to acknowledge what the other person is saying by nodding, smiling, making eye contact, or uttering something like "uh-huh."
- The third step is to ensure that you understand the content of what the other person is saying and that you can restate the ideas in a way that satisfies the other person that you understand.
- The fourth step is listening for the emotions that are felt by the other party. Invariably, if the topic you are discussing is important, there is some emotion wrapped around the main ideas. Or, more accurately, it is often embedded deep inside where it isn't always obvious, but being hidden does not diminish its influence.
- The fifth level of good listening involves your taking some action that is appropriate, given the message that you've heard.

Inspirational leaders who want to use their emotions to influence others will ideally begin by finding out what others are feeling. This enables them to select the most helpful messages given the circumstances.

One secret to being inspirational is to be effective on both the sending and the receiving side of emotions.

> A colleague of ours, Carolyn Larkin, runs a group of consultancies in Latin America. One evening she told us the story of an adopted daughter in her family. This girl was in the car with her parents when the car was involved in a horrible accident in which both of her parents were killed instantly. She was then sent by her family to live with an aunt and uncle who had agreed to raise her. Within a matter of months, the aunt was stricken with a

rapidly invasive cancer and passed away weeks after the diagnosis was made.

Carolyn Larkin was related to the girl and agreed to have her come to live with her and her husband and be adopted by them. As this happened, Carolyn began thinking about this young girl, now 11 years old, and the life experiences she had endured.

On the first night of her being in her new home, Carolyn took her into a bedroom and said, "We must have a serious talk. I want you to be very clear about something. You need to understand that if anything were ever to happen to me—a sickness or an accident—you would have nothing to with that. You would in no way be responsible for that happening. Do you understand what I'm saying?" The girl broke into tears and sobbed for several minutes. At last someone had had the sensitivity to understand the feelings that had mistakenly welled up inside her and to also anticipate her worst nightmare. She was now released from any responsibility that a naïve young mind would concoct.

The girl grew up to be a fully functioning, happy women engaged in a successful career. One of the important gifts she received was an adoptive parent with the ability to anticipate a potentially damaging emotion. This remarkable act of sensitivity to the feelings of another person illustrates one of the qualities of inspirational leaders. They are attuned to the emotions of others.

BECOME MORE EXTROVERTED

That's easier said than done, right? It is tempting to adhere to the party line of most behavioral scientists, who say that there is no right way to behave. This viewpoint contends that we're all unique and that we should all simply respect the differences we possess. But the fact of the matter is that if a person wants to be more inspirational in more circumstances, that person needs to act in a more extro-verted way more of the time.

We've all heard interviews with actors and actresses who confess to being quite shy. By nature, many of these performers prefer to hang back and let others do the talking. But they've also learned how to act the part of the extrovert and to deal with whatever internal discomfort they experience in doing that.

The evidence is very clear. The extrovert has more influence and provides more inspiration than the introvert. This means that you need to be the one who says "hello" to the person in the hall, not wait for that person to speak to you. You need to extend your hand, not wait for the other person. You invite the loner who is outside the circle to come and join your group. You get up and move out of the safe haven that is your office to meet other people in their offices. Extroverts speak loudly and confidently enough for others to easily hear them.

The entire process of emotional contagion depends on the degree to which you behave in a more extroverted manner. So, if that isn't your natural style, we encourage you to start working on it.

One final comment is extremely important, however. Can intro-verts be inspirational? Yes. They can express interest and concern for others. They can praise. They can provide helpful feedback. There are myriad ways for an introvert to be inspirational. They will simply miss out on the additional acts of inspiration that the extrovert achieves.

One of the underlying messages of focusing on others is to not focus so much on yourself. Think about what you do in conversa-tions that makes other people feel that they are the only people of importance in the room. That means that you can't be looking around the room, scanning the scene to see if there is someone more important for you to be talking to.

DISPLAY YOUR EMOTIONS WITH GREATER AMPLITUDE AND FREQUENCY

We all know people who have a "poker" face. You have no idea what they are feeling or thinking. Then we know people who seem to be completely transparent. You know when they are troubled, just as you can tell when they are happy or excited. It should come as no surprise that the most inspiring leaders are those on the transparent side. They are expressive. And the research is especially clear about the power of expressing positive emotions through your facial expressions and body language.

- *Amplitude.* The effective leader does not hesitate to state opinions with an extra dose of emphasis. The leader knows that ideas that are expressed with vigor and with powerful words will have more effect. So, don't hold back. Don't hesitate to make your messages strong.
- *Frequency.* Powerful messages need to be delivered frequently. When people hear the same message for the seventh time, it becomes clear to them that the leader is very committed to this idea.
- *Drama.* Use dramatic, unconventional behavior.

   An executive wanted to send a message to the organization about the need to cut bureaucracy and waste. The executive believed that there were an excessive number of reports and approval processes. Unnecessary paperwork had become a giant barnacle on the hull of the organization. So he came into a "town hall" type meeting where senior and middle managers were assembled. On a table next to the podium was a large collection of reports. After introducing the topic and expressing his concern and his fervent hope that this group would take prompt action, the executive pulled out a large machete from behind the podium and proceeded to hack these reports into pieces. (He'd covered the table with a piece of plywood.) Some members of the group sat in stunned silence and others started chuckling, but no one could mistake the message or forget the imagery. It worked. The group clearly got the message because of this dramatic image of reports being hacked up.

- *Take personal risks.*

   It is always impressive to see the leaders of an organization get outside their comfort zone. The CEO of Marriott

Corporation, Bill Marriott, has recently begun a personal blog as a way of connecting with the vast number of Marriott customers and employees. It happens that Bill comes from a generation that isn't totally comfortable with computers, and he isn't one to handle his own e-mail. However, a new communications vice president convinced him that having his own blog could have a positive effect. He writes quite personal things, such as how he and his wife go to the movies on Saturday afternoon, buy a large bucket of popcorn, and hold hands during the movie. Readers have responded to these personal messages with great enthusiasm, somewhat to his surprise.

PHYSICALLY ACT THE PART

The following professional behaviors may seem like a list of mundane actions. Many of them are obvious to most people. But they are still critical to leadership.

- Look people in the eye when you speak with them.
- Stand up straight. Good posture conveys pride, discipline, and confidence.
- Practice a firm but not bone-crushing handshake. A handshake sounds like a trivial thing, but we've heard it talked about as the reason why an executive wasn't selected for a position.
- Relax. When interacting with others, do your best to be at ease so that you can focus on others.
- Dress well. Fit in with the group, but don't be underdressed unless you work for Apple Computer.
- Smile. A smile is an emotion made visible. The most inspiring people are those with the capacity to smile. Leaving your politics aside, think of the presidents of the United States who inspired the nation the most. We would mention Eisenhower, Kennedy, Reagan, and Clinton. Each had an engaging smile that was accompanied by self-deprecating humor.

IMPROVE YOUR ONE-ON-ONE INTERACTIONS

Much of a leader's day is spent in interactions with colleagues. These provide an opportunity for the leader to begin and end the conversation with a positive, uplifting comment. Often that can be one of appreciation for what your colleague is doing for the organization. When such conversations provide specific and detailed appreciation for what this person has done and it is made personal ("I want you to know how much I appreciate what you are doing for the organization."), this message moves from being perfunctory to being very inspirational to the recipient.

PRACTICE WORKING A ROOM

The phrase "work the room" has taken on highly negative connotations for many of us. It smacks of something contrived and manipulative, maybe even a bit phony. To many it feels superficial.

Let's look at the other side for a moment. We're all caught in large gatherings on occasion. Some people are extremely uncomfortable in this situation, so they latch on to one person and spend the entire time talking with that individual. Does that describe you?

Would it not have been better if you had moved about, connecting with many of those in attendance? Could you have met new people, learned their names, made newcomers to the organization feel more at home, and had a positive influence on a dozen or more, rather than only one? Moving about in a large gathering is not just for politicians and schmoozers. It is for leaders who want to be inspirational.

SET THE TONE FOR TEAM MEETINGS

Every team meeting is a perfect opportunity for the leader to be inspirational. Leaders make the team feel that it is something out of the ordinary and set apart from all the others. The leader's participation will usually set the tone of the meeting. Others will take their cue from the leader.

If the leader uses the meeting to take cheap shots and publicly criticize, others will follow suit. If the leader delights in antagonistic confrontation, that's where every meeting will head.

If the leader uses the meeting to highlight positive accomplishments, to openly bring to the surface challenges that the group is facing, and to engage in collaborative problem solving, the meeting has now become extremely productive and valuable. If the leader keeps the tone highly constructive and the conversation honest, then the meeting will be inspirational to all who attend.

> One of the authors attended a large gathering of leaders from the Adidas organization. The meeting was held in Kuala Lumpur and was labeled a Collaboration Summit. The organization was bringing together four brands (Adidas, Rockport, Reebok, and Taylor Made) and was seeking to obtain greater synergy in all the countries in that region. More than 450 people attended the session. The tone was one of celebration of their amazing success in pulling these organizations together in a relatively short time and the positive impact that this was having on the organization. Part of the meeting was devoted to teams working on the remaining challenges of making the integration work smoothly. Executives spoke warmly about the efforts of the people in the room. The meeting combined learning, problem solving, and fun. While there were still some hurdles to be overcome, this part of the organization was showing the rest of the company what could be done when people truly collaborated.

IMPROVE YOUR PUBLIC SPEAKING SKILLS
Manner

An experiment was conducted in which a businessperson presented a long-range vision to an assembled group. Then a professional actor presented the same vision to a different, but similar group. The second presentation was much more warmly received. Why? The content was exactly the same. What is it that professional actors do that a nonactor does not do?

Our observation would be that the actor varies the pace. He isn't afraid to insert long pauses. He treats words as if they were jewels on a velvet pad with a bright light shining on them. Important phrases are given greater emphasis through loudness or softness of voice and varying pitch. When possible, the actor tells stories. Actors know that the audience will remember the story because it is the perfect vehicle to convey emotion.

When you speak, lean forward. Look at all parts of the room. Spend a few seconds looking intently at one person and then move to someone in a different place. Use gestures that have the palms of your hands moving forward or upward.

Most of us don't aspire to completely emulate professional actors, but there are some lessons to be learned from them. They understand that real communication involves a thought that is carefully wrapped with some emotion. The actor works hard to send both parts of the message, realizing that both are extremely important to the hearer.

We would remind the reader that subordinates want to know your ideas, but at the same time they want to know how you really feel about those ideas. Effective communication must convey both.

Content

While a later chapter in this book will deal with the leader as a communicator and with the power of goals and vision statements, we want to acknowledge the importance of content, lest the reader believe that we care only about delivery and style. The forward-thinking, expansive vision statement is very inspiring when it is presented well. Such messages create a healthy cognitive dissonance because they describe where the organization could and should be, and compare it to today's reality. That discrepancy sets up powerful forces that begin the change process. A compelling vision provides a source of inspiration to those who believe that it is realistic and that you are really committed to achieving it.

When the leader talks of a future that includes growth, new products, new facilities, expanded customer lists, and a growing number of associates; a number of important messages are being conveyed. These are messages of trust, optimism, confidence, and hope.

> George Bernard Shaw's play *Pygmalion* portrays a young Cockney girl who is taken in by a professor of speech who teaches her to act and talk in the manner of a dignified lady. While the relationship between the professor and the girl is complicated, there is an enormous message of trust sent by the professor to the girl regarding her ability to transform herself. She ultimately learns to speak and act in the appropriate ways.

Moving beyond the status quo is inspiring. A willingness to take a controversial stand on an important topic is inspirational. The content of your message accompanies the way it is delivered, and together they unite to create inspiration.

HELP THE PEOPLE WHO WORK WITH YOU TO BE HAPPY

As one prominent researcher noted, "Perhaps the most important resource-building human trait is productivity at work (better known as 'getting it out the door')."[8] He goes on to note that "happier people are markedly more satisfied with their jobs than less happy people" and that "happiness causes more productivity."

What causes employee happiness? A big factor is the leader. A variety of researchers have conclusively shown that charismatic or inspiring leaders use their strong emotions to arouse exactly those same positive emotions in their followers.[9] This has been dubbed a process of "emotional contagion," and the more formal the role of the leader, the more powerfully leaders pass on positive emotions to others. One researcher studied a group of sales managers. In this carefully controlled field study, it was obvious that when the leader was in a positive mood, this mood was passed on to the group. This elevation of mood and emotion in turn became a strong predictor of the group's performance.[10]

CONCLUSION

Inspiration and emotion are inextricably linked together. The inspiring leader learns how to use this other realm of life, despite the fact that we seldom have any formal education or training that would help us to be good at it. The fact is that the proper use of emotion is a key factor in the success of every inspiring leader.

While most leaders have had little in the way of formal assistance in how to navigate in these waters, some facts about the use of emotion are becoming quite clear. We've presented those in this chapter. As we learn more, the mystery of inspiration diminishes. We're getting a reasonably clear handle on what leaders do that inspires their followers.

Many of us attend to extreme emotions. We are quick to respond when people become extremely angry, sad, or joyful. What we're less effective at doing is being attentive to the more subtle, nuanced emotions that exist below our radar screen. These tip us off to impending issues. Many of us need to become more attuned to our own moods and emotions.

Most of all, we need to get comfortable doing the things that inspiring leaders know and do so well. In general, these behaviors are not that difficult. They push some people outside of their comfort zone, but performing them becomes its own reward. We're almost always immediately repaid with positive reinforcement when we practice the behaviors of the inspiring leader.

STEPS TO TAKE

1. Assess your own comfort with the world of emotion. Are you usually aware of when your colleagues are feeling down or elated? Do you know why?
2. Tune in to your own emotions. Become more attuned to your own moods. Acknowledge when you are out of sorts and other people are tiptoeing around you.
   - If you are having a bad day, limit your interactions with others.

- If you are having a good day, expand your interactions. Reach out to people more.
- If you tend to be more pessimistic than optimistic, find ways to focus on what's right and spend less time on what's wrong. Look for what people are doing that is positive rather than mistakes that they make or flat sides that they have.

3. Be attuned to the emotions of those about you. During your conversations with others, let them know that you are aware of their reaction to a decision or situation, whether it be anger, disappointment, excitement, surprise, frustration, or pride.

4. Become more extroverted.
   - Initiate conversations and be the one to extend a hand or say "hello."
   - Speak loudly and confidently enough that others can hear you.
   - Go to others' offices.
   - Work on making an "emotional" or "human" connection with everyone you meet.
   - Reveal more of yourself.
   - Keep a smile on your face rather than a worried frown.

5. Display your emotions with greater amplitude and frequency.
   - Express positive emotions through your facial expressions and body language.
   - Amplitude. Don't hesitate to state your opinions with added emphasis.
   - Frequency. Deliver powerful messages frequently.
   - Drama. Use dramatic, unconventional behavior. If there is an important message that you think your group needs to hear, find some way to convey it in a truly memorable way.
   - Take personal risks.
   - Step outside your comfort zone.

6. Physically act the part.
   - Look people in the eye when you speak with them.
   - Stand up straight.
   - Practice a firm but not bone-crushing handshake.

- Relax.
- Dress well.
- Smile.
- Put a twinkle in your eye.
7. Improve your one-on-one interactions.
   - Begin and end conversations with positive and uplifting comments.
   - Personalize what you say to your employees.
8. Practice making good use of large gatherings. Move around the room, learning and remembering names.
9. Set the tone for team meetings.
   - Does your participation set the tone for the meeting?
   - Be constructive and keep the conversation honest.
   - Observe the emotional tone of your staff meetings. Is it glum? Do people come either grudgingly or with an air of resignation at putting up with this period of mild torture? Or is there an excitement and cheer in the air? What could you do to begin every meeting with something that sets a positive tone? How about going around the room and having people report on some positive event that happened during the prior period?
10. Improve your public speaking skills.
    - Vary the pace and pitch of your voice.
    - Use pauses and look at people in different parts of the room.
    - Lean forward and use hand gestures.
    - Tell stories.
11. Help the people who work with you to be happy.
    - Use your strong emotions to arouse the same positive emotions in others.

Chapter 7

Setting Stretch Goals

I am here for a purpose and that purpose is to grow into a mountain, not to shrink to a grain of sand. I will strain my potential until it cries for mercy.

—Og Mandino

Make no little plans. They have no magic to stir men's blood and probably themselves will not be realized. Make big plans, aim high in hope and work, remembering that a noble, logical diagram once recorded will not die.

—Daniel H. Burnham

When people describe an extraordinary experience at work, most of the time this experience involves an objective that was extremely challenging and complex. Often the goal was so challenging that they were not certain that it could be accomplished. People often relate a fascinating story that describes how they applied their skills, knowledge, and experience together with hard work. Add to that some luck, and the goal was accomplished. If you ask people about their work satisfaction during this difficult but extraordinary experience, they invariably describe this as a time when they were extremely satisfied. They go on to describe it as a time when they were extremely productive. If you ask them how they felt about themselves during the experience, the answer is that they felt confident, self-assured, positive, and enthusiastic. If you ask them about their work-life balance during this period, many say that it was out of balance from the perspective of personal time, but that this didn't seem to matter that much because when they were not working, they felt so good about what they were accomplishing professionally that it made what personal time they had better as well.

Over the last few years, this paradox has become very clear to us: while many people tend to resist taking on difficult, challenging assignments, they are most happy and fulfilled when they accomplish a stretch goal. The bottom line seems to be that if you want to make people feel extremely fulfilled, give them challenging work in which they can be successful.

When you think about the backbreaking pace that many people endure at work and ask these people what they would prefer to be doing, they talk about the beach, relaxation, or "chilling out." But rest and relaxation, while fulfilling for a short time, eventually lead people to boredom. The vacation we remember the most is seldom the one in which we sat and did nothing. Leaders who can get their team members to take on challenging and difficult assignments that can be accomplished end up with team members who are the most highly satisfied, productive, and fulfilled.

The formula here is that leaders who can get people to take on challenging assignments at which they can be successful will have team members who are highly satisfied and more productive. This, in turn, helps the leader to be viewed as more inspirational. This is a self-perpetuating cycle.

LOFTY GOALS

Inspirational leaders believe that the organization is capable of producing at a higher level than it is at the current time. Jack Welch often observed about human performance that "there's no end to the juice in that lemon." The truth of the matter is that when there is a crisis or when some event triggers it, groups nearly always become capable of performing at a much higher level.

Peter Drucker wrote: "The single greatest challenge facing managers in the developed countries of the world is to raise the productivity of knowledge and service workers. This challenge, which will dominate the management agenda for the next several decades, will ultimately determine the competitive performance of companies."

Look at the scoring pattern in most athletic contests. The number of points scored in the final minutes of a football game is enormously higher than during any other period. People rise to the occasion when they are highly motivated.

Along with a belief that the group can produce more, the leader must also be discontented with the status quo. For whatever reasons, the leader must feel a strong need for things to change. It could be because of a new competitor. It could be because the leader believes that more difficult times are coming in the economy. Or it could be that the leader recognizes that because it can be done, it should be done. Period.

CONCLUSIONS FROM RESEARCH

Our research revealed some specific actions that leaders engaged in to set lofty goals.

At the Core of Setting Lofty Goals Are the Leader's Courage and Willingness to Take On Risk

When leaders consider setting a lofty, difficult stretch goal, many of them will have an unpleasant feeling deep in the pit of their stomach. Thoughts will come to their mind, including:

- This is not a 100 percent sure thing.
- I will be taking a personal risk.
- No one has done this before.
- What is going to happen if it fails?
- Can I get the team to accept this challenge?

While it is difficult to teach people to have more courage, we want to acknowledge that courage is a fundamental part of the process. Setting lofty goals will never be easy and will never be without some risk. We can, however, provide two assurances. First, we know that people invariably have a lot more that they can give. One study estimated that on average, employees waste 1.44 hours each day on nonproductive activities.[1] Beyond that, employees who just go through the motions in doing their job never produce the kind of superior results that they are capable of producing. In a study of more than 100,000 employees who were asked if their work environment encouraged people to "go the extra mile," only 29 percent of the employees strongly agreed, and 26 percent responded to that question with a neutral or negative reply. (This is instructive, because the question simply asked if the work environment encouraged that type of behavior. It didn't ask if people actually went the extra mile.) That analysis indicates that at least a quarter of employees go through the motions each day but are not highly committed to putting forth their best efforts.

Second, small increases in productivity can have profound effects. We mentioned in an earlier chapter that Peter Drucker observed that if an average company increased productivity by only 10 percent, it would double its profits. (The average firm produces approximately 5 percent after-tax profits. The S&P 500 earn slightly more than that, and other firms generally earn less. People costs are usually the largest line item for firms, but there are obviously huge differences.) If the firm's productivity gains were 5 percent, then it would have half again as much profit.

While discussing Drucker's observation in many different companies, we have found a consistent reaction. The first reaction that people have is often skepticism. It simply sounds too good to be true. But, after they consider their people costs, their profit margin, and the fact that most of the time an increase in employee productivity would not add any additional cost, they come to the same conclusion. You can almost hear them say in unison, "It would all go to the bottom line." While many lofty goals seem like a great deal of effort, a little bit of effort from a lot of people often gets those goals accomplished.

Have the Confidence to Get Team Members to Embrace a New Reality

People determine their own limitations and expectations. Leaders who are working with a team with the aim of having the team members embrace a stretch goal need to approach that process with a great deal of energy and commitment. Any hesitation or doubt on the part of the leader can quickly open the door to a mutiny. After discussing stretch goals with a number of leaders, it has become clear to us that while their public persona displayed incredible confidence, the goal was often determined by an educated guess.

> Pete was in charge of an effort to downsize a large manufacturing organization. While the company was still profitable, margins were slipping, raw materials costs were increasing, and competition was making it impossible for the company to raise prices. A small group of senior managers met to discuss the downsizing goal. The accountants indicated that 12 percent of the cost needed to be taken out in order to retain the desired level of productivity. Pete asked for one week to study this issue and return with a decision.
>
> In a week Pete returned to the meeting. He said that after looking at a great deal of data and having numerous discussions, he had determined that the goal for the downsizing was 25 percent. You could hear people gasp. In unison people said, "That's impossible—you'll destroy the business." Pete took on all the questions. He remained calm but totally committed to 25 percent.
>
> Over the next three months, Pete met with group after group who said that 25 percent was impossible, but he simply sent them back and asked them to sharpen their pencils. No group escaped the reduction. By four months, every group in the company had figured out a way to accomplish its goal. The downsizing went smoothly, and Pete was a real hero. In an interview a year

after the event, Pete was asked how he determined the number. "It was my best guess," he replied. "I knew that we had it in many places, and I knew that whatever the number was, no group would give me more than that number. So, after thinking about it for several days, I just decided that we could do 25 percent. I figured that if that was too much, someone would convince me that I was wrong, and that never happened."

Involvement Is the Key to Raising the Bar

Somehow the leader must raise the bar. There are many ways to do that. One approach is illustrated by the sales manager who calls a salesperson into the office and simply announces that the quota for that territory is being increased by 20 percent. The sales manager may then give some rationale for that, such as increasing prices, expansion of clients, or changes in the economy—all in an attempt to make the salesperson accept and feel good about the new quota. But this approach is fundamentally unilateral. Is that a good approach?

The American Productivity Council reports that only 2.5 percent of companies surveyed believed that management-initiated changes were the most important source of improved performance. On the other hand, 62 percent identified employees as the most important source of those ideas. To have the employees become the source of the ideas, the leader would have to behave in an extremely different manner. Here's an example.

The sales manager could meet with the salesperson regarding the need to arrive at a new quota for the coming year. This discussion might begin with a review together of the available data and with the sales manager seeking the salesperson's ideas. (All this assumes that raising the target for the salesperson doesn't have a negative financial impact on him. If it does have a negative impact, there will nearly always be greater resistance.)

Is this always a better approach? We suspect it depends on many factors. The high school swimming coach who has her young swimmers swim 20 laps in an Olympic-sized pool on the first day of practice is setting the bar at a higher level than most high school students would have chosen for themselves. In some circumstances, the leader may be required to raise the bar in a somewhat unilateral way. That continues through much of high school and college. Teachers and professors believe students to be capable of doing things that most of the students would find hard to believe.

The Fremont Swim Club in northern California produced a long series of winning swim teams, including many swimmers who went on to participate in the Olympics. The coaches had a wonderful knack of pushing young swimmers until they reached their maximum performance, and then knowing how to back off a bit or jumping into the pool themselves to break the tension.

As time passes, however, that same approach may not be the ideal one for the more experienced worker. At that stage, it seems far more appropriate to make important decisions in partnership between two adults, and not as a parent to a child. In most leadership situations involving mature adults who bring experience to their work, a joint problem-solving discussion works far better than a unilateral command.

One of the important contributions a leader makes is to expand the thinking of the subordinate about what can be accomplished and how it might be done. An important leadership principle is that the leader should be extremely clear about the outcome that is expected, but should leave a great deal of wiggle room for the employee in terms of how the task is completed. Often the employee doesn't have as much experience as the leader. The employee hasn't seen anyone attempt this task, or anything remotely like it. Here's where the leader, after exhausting all the employee's ideas, can suggest other approaches to consider.

Make Sure That Your Lofty Goal Is Not Unreasonable—Lofty Goals Need to Be Realistic

Most people are aware that when they set stretch goals, their performance improves. In many organizations this has become a way of life, but some leaders take the principle to an extreme by setting impossible goals. At least, the goal seems impossible to the people who need to embrace and execute it. When this occurs, it has the opposite effect from inspiring people. Instead, it demotivates people. They start to attribute ulterior motives to the leader who sets impossible goals. They view the leader as a greedy taskmaster whose only motive is more profit. There is a fine art to setting stretch goals that others will embrace. Ultimately, the issues are that people need to believe in their ability to achieve the goal and that there always needs to be some worthy purpose for the goal.

The employees are also going to expect the leader to lead by creating the conditions that will allow the new targets to be met. If the leader is unwilling to do that, the employee group will soon question the seriousness of this new target. One barrier in many organizations is the stifling bureaucracy that often gets in the way of getting things done. Peter Drucker observed, "Most of what we call management consists of things that make it increasingly difficult for the workers to get their jobs done." The manager must be willing to banish bureaucracy and remove the barriers to high productivity.

An extreme expression of that perspective came from a Russian plant manager, Vladimir Karaidze, of the Ivanovo Machine Building Works near Moscow. His plant had been plagued with excessive bureaucratic requirements for forms and paperwork. He wrote to a colleague in Moscow, "I can't stand this proliferation of paperwork. It is useless to fight the forms. You've got to kill the people producing them." Most people with experience in organizations can share and feel his frustration, but hope he was joking about the solution.

A Key to Accomplishing Lofty Goals Is to Follow Through and Then Follow Through Some More

Some leaders set a lofty goal for their team and ask for the team's dedicated effort and commitment. In a few months, these same leaders go to the team with a new goal and again ask for the team members' dedication and commitment. Such leaders simply fail to stay the course. Everyone knows how this story continues: changing priorities month after month, along with new commitments. It becomes the flavor of the month. What employees learn to do is to sandbag each of these commitments, look very busy, and conserve as much energy as possible. The consensus among the employees is that if you wait long enough, the leader will forget about previous commitments in the rush to the next goal. One person explained his approach in the following way.

> When my boss has an assignment, I go to his office and take careful notes. I ask lots of questions and document exactly what is wanted and how it should be done. I always tell the boss that I will get right on this new assignment. Then I go to my office, file the notes, and do nothing. Most of the time my boss just forgets about what he asked me to do, but sometimes I get a call and a request for a progress report. I tell him that I need a couple of days to pull everything together and I will give him a progress report. I then pull out my notes and work very hard to make some progress. When I do a progress report, I always give him some critical decisions that he needs to make to keep the project moving forward. It's not that I am lazy. I am working 60 to 70 hours a week and barely holding my head above water. This is the only way that I can survive.

One of the most frequent complaints from employees is that priorities are constantly changing. Everyone needs a clear line of sight about which work is critical and which is a lower priority.

For many leaders, the key to keeping their team focused on the most important priorities is that they must be willing to push back on new priorities that come from senior leaders. We are not suggesting that leaders be insubordinate, but they need to understand how a new priority fits with last month's priorities.

Benchmark Your Organization to Other High-Performing Organizations

One of the popular techniques that leaders used in the early years of the Total Quality Management movement was to send their employees to visit other organizations that had a reputation for doing something extremely well. Xerox sent a team of people who were working on a process to speed distribution of its products to Domino's Pizza, an early pioneer in speedy delivery of its product. Benchmarking was a powerful way to get employees to see for themselves a better way to approach a task, without the leader's being the one to go collect the information and bring it back to the group.

As organizations mature, an attitude of "we know best" or "this is how we've always done it" often creeps in. This "we know it all" attitude is the antithesis of the "learning organization" that is actively looking for new and better ways.

Leaders often initiate discussions about performance with individuals when there is an obvious problem. This could include things not being done on time. Or it could be that tasks are being accomplished in a less than professional manner. Often the leader may raise these performance deficiencies with the entire team in a staff meeting.

But is that the only time to have performance discussions? What if the leader initiated a performance discussion with the team when things were going quite well? What if the leader asked for the team members' ideas about how things could be even better? *This is a leadership act of the highest order.*

Think of how you might initiate such a conversation with your group.

Identify Peak Performers in the Organization

One powerful technique that leaders use is to ferret out the individuals already within the organization who are unusually fast or good at what they do. For some reason, these people are often ignored, and their improved processes and techniques help them to perform well personally, but are never adopted by others. When high performers are not recognized or rewarded for their exceptional performance, their performance will usually gradually decline.

Worse yet is when leaders single out their favorites and ignore every other individual or team. When trying to improve the performance of any group of individuals or any team, a good question to ask is, "Which individuals (or what teams) are doing this extremely well? Let's identify these people or teams and seek their permission to observe them, interview them, and have them become the trainers for new people coming in."

Utilize Team Dynamics and Support to Achieve Stretch Goals

Many leaders have discovered that having the team set its goals collectively can be a powerful technique. Invariably, one or more of the team members would like to reach higher. They toss out potential goals that the manager would be wary of proposing, but having such a goal come from one of the team members makes it infinitely more appealing. Many managers have found themselves in the position of attempting to scale back the team's ambitions. That's usually a much more favorable position than trying to radically lift the sights of individuals or the team. We encourage leaders to experiment with this technique. Prior to a team meeting in which you toss the challenge of establishing a goal or target for the completion of a project to the team, write down what you would have proposed had you done this unilaterally. Then compare that to what the team decides on.

Why does this succeed so frequently? We know that people support decisions that they helped to make. When the team has an active part in the decision process, everyone on the team is more committed to making it succeed. The acceptance of a decision is a huge part of its success, and having the team make the decision collectively adds one more important dimension. Now the team members are holding one another accountable for doing what is required to meet the target that they collectively set.

Improve Processes and Remove Bureaucracy

Another technique that leaders use to raise the bar is to challenge individuals or teams to streamline the processes that they use. Seldom do you find complex systems in organizations that can't be improved if people will take the time to map out the current process in some detail, then look for places to eliminate unnecessary steps or generally streamline the entire process.

The airline industry has saved millions of dollars by moving from paper tickets to e-tickets. Direct deposit payroll checks have been a real boon to both corporations and their employees.

In order to really improve processes, people need to ask more lofty questions. Getting a 10 percent increase in productivity on a process can typically be done by people just working a little bit harder. Asking for a 50 percent improvement forces the team to consider entirely new approaches. Bureaucracy is often so embedded that it is considered off limits to change or improvement. Great leaders look everywhere for opportunities.

Celebration and Reward

Regardless of how committed your team is, if a lofty goal is achieved, celebration and rewards for the individuals and the team need to be carefully considered. Teams have to celebrate victories—even at important milestones along the way to the ultimate goal. Of course, most organizations are not finished when a major objective is reached. In fact, most of the time, that objective is quickly followed by yet another. So when it is time for the team members to give all that they can for the next hard-to-achieve goal, they need to look back and feel that they were appropriately recognized and rewarded for their extra effort and performance. Otherwise, why would they do it again? Stretch goals deserve stretch rewards and ought to be celebrated in a way that is appropriate for your organization.

CONCLUSION

Most people are willing to put forth a reasonable amount of effort, but at some point they hold back and look for ways to conserve energy. We probably learn this from our physical limitations. After you have been holding your breath for a period of time, the instinct and desire to breathe are very strong. Even though most people could hold their breath longer, the instinct wins out. For most of us, when we are asked the question, "Did you give all that you had to give?" the honest answer is no. There is a great deal of conserved energy in every organization. Setting stretch goals can release some of that conserved energy, bringing increased productivity and success to the organization. The great side effect of getting people to stretch is that when people accomplish challenging objectives, they are happier about their jobs and more pleased with themselves.

After reading this chapter, some people may assume that all team members will be overjoyed at being given a very challenging objective. However, those with experience know they will not be. There will often be some complaints, groans, and criticism of the leader. But if you follow the principles outlined in this chapter, this could eventually be one of the best memories people have and something that fills them with pride and confidence for years to come.

STEPS TO TAKE

1. Review the work assignments of those reporting to you and ask the question, "Are these assignments challenging?" Then determine how these assignments could be made even more fulfilling.
2. Believe that your organization is capable of producing at a higher level than it is doing at the current time. Think of what could happen if a crisis arose. What could your team accomplish?
3. Discuss with your team its ideas for exciting new goals to which the team members would aspire. Involve them in defining ways to raise the bar.

4. Make sure your lofty goal is not unreasonable. Do your people believe that it is realistic? What do they see as the barriers to attaining it? Which of these barriers must you remove?

5. Stick to goals until they are realized. Keep previous commitments and expectations alive and in perspective with anything new that is added.

6. Benchmark your organization to other high-performing organizations. Implement what works well for other businesses in your organization.

7. Identify peak performers in the organization. Give praise and make an example of those in your organization who are unusually fast or good at what they do.

8. Utilize team dynamics and support to achieve stretch goals. Have your team collectively set goals.

9. Improve processes and remove bureaucracy. Encourage individuals and teams to streamline processes.

10. Celebration and reward. Celebrate and recognize the achievement of goals and milestones. Plan frequent celebrations and rewards.

For additional free resources on how to set stretch goals with your team please refer to www.zengerfolkman.com and click on the Inspiring Leader icon.

Chapter 8

Creating Vision and Direction

Vision without action is a daydream. Action without vision is a nightmare.

—Japanese Proverb

The only limits are, as always, those of vision.

—James Broughton

Leadership is not a magnetic personality—that can just as well be a glib tongue. It is not "making friends and influencing people"—that is flattery. Leadership is lifting a person's vision to high sights, the raising of a person's performance to a higher standard, the building of a personality beyond its normal limitations.

—Peter Drucker

Inspiring leaders excel at creating vision and providing clear direction to the people about them. In the spirit of this attribute, we will paint the total picture of this leadership behavior at the very beginning, then treat each of the parts in greater detail.

THE PROCESS OF CREATING CLEAR VISION AND DIRECTION

Here's how the leader goes about creating greater clarity of vision and direction:

1. The leader orchestrates a process that creates a concise, compelling, and clear vision for the organization. This is not a "solo" activity for the leader. Leaders ought not to think that it

is incumbent upon them to have the answer. Nor does this need to be for an entire corporation. Middle managers in any functional area can do this for the group they lead.

2. This vision combines a strong statement of the guiding principles that shape the organization with a vivid picture of what it aspires to be in the next few years. Don't confuse having a vision and providing clarity of direction with having a mission statement. The vision is not a "forever" picture, as a mission statement tends to be.

3. With this vision clearly stated, a clear line of sight can now be established between each individual's work and where the organization wants to go. This enables all individuals to be engaged in day-to-day activities with a clear sense of direction and purpose and a knowledge of how what they do fits into the larger picture. Work now takes on greater meaning.

4. This clarity of direction also resolves questions about what is trivial and what is titanic. A clear vision and direction for the organization also defines on a daily basis what should be ignored or put on the back burner. Individuals can then stay focused on the most important activities and issues.

5. All systems and new initiatives can now be brought into alignment around the vision.

6. Effective strategies and optimum tactics flow more easily from this clearer vision for the organization.

WHY DOES THIS CREATE MORE INSPIRED AND MOTIVATED COLLEAGUES?

At the most fundamental level, providing clear vision and direction is a tangible expression of the leader's treating other people in the organization with dignity and respect.

If a group of adults decided to go on a hike together, chances are that the person who was nominally in charge would ask the people in the group to look at a map and would indicate the planned destination and the route by which the group would collectively get there. Imagine how frustrating it would be if the group were asked to simply follow the leader. In essence, the leader would be saying, "I know where we're going; I'll lead you there. You don't need to know anything more than that." Worse yet, after stopping for lunch, imagine the frustration that the group would feel if the leader meandered off in different directions, apparently looking for the most appealing path, but consulted with no one in that process.

Such a scenario would trigger images of the worst scenes from a *Dilbert* cartoon. The consequences of this behavior would be the disdain and apathy that are not so subtly displayed by the characters in that comic strip. We'll refer to the situation just described as Scenario A.

Now imagine Scenario B. This leader asks the group to convene and describes a potential destination. But now the leader asks if everyone thinks that this is a good destination and, only after getting agreement on its being a good target, asks for any thoughts about the best way of getting there. One person in the group has made this hike before and offers some useful suggestions about one area to avoid because the trail is muddy at this time of year. Another person notices a lake and offers to bring a fishing pole to provide fresh fish for the group lunch. Before the group leaves, everyone is clear about the destination. A time to stop for lunch has been agreed on by the group, and then they embark on the hike. As they begin to hike, one part of the group challenges the rest of the group to a race, which results in some people reaching the goal much sooner than the others. But rather than complaining about having to wait for the others or about their strained muscles, the group is energized, happy, and ready for another adventure.

It is completely obvious which scenario would create a higher level of motivation for the hikers. The first group would experience considerable mumbling and grousing, while the second group would travel in relative harmony.

STEPS IN CREATING CLEAR VISION AND DIRECTION
Orchestrate a Process by Which a Plan Is Defined

The first thing to emphasize is that the leader does not go off and come back with a vision that he created all alone. Visions that inspire need not be solo endeavors. Yes, the entrepreneur of a start-up organization may have strong ideas about what she would like to accomplish, but for most organizations, this ideally is a collaborative process.

Note also that this is not always done first by the most senior executive in the organization. While most people would agree that this is the ideal place to begin, the reality is that visions are created for divisions, departments, and functions in the organization. Their influence usually radiates in all directions and encourages others to do the same.

Make Sure the Vision Captures the Important Guiding Principles

This includes the values that drive the organization. The vision should add a vivid picture of what the organization aspires to be. The important qualities are that it is

- Clear
- Compelling
- Concrete
- Succinct
- Engaging
- Visceral

Consider two examples from different realms. Many people attend car shows in which manufacturers of automobiles display their latest models. They also display concept cars that herald what is to come. Features from these concept cars, depending on public reaction and the feasibility of manufacturing them, can end up on production cars in just a few years.

A second example is the unveiling of a model by the architects who are aspiring to win the bid for a major new building. At the appropriate moment, the model of the building is uncovered. With painstaking detail, the building has been created in miniature and placed in its context, often surrounded by miniature trees and cars. Suddenly the concept of the building takes on life.

In each case, there could have been an oral description of the car or the building. Or, going to the next step, there could have been dimensional drawings showing front views, side views, and top-down perspectives.

The creation of models comes at considerable expense for the auto manufacturer. And while the model of the building is less costly, the creation of the miniature building is not a trivial under-taking. But in each case the model takes something that could be abstract and makes it clear, compelling, and concrete. People develop some visceral reaction as they are either drawn to or repelled by what they see.

In describing the vision for a corporation or some portion of it, there is an obvious challenge. Corporations are by definition a cre-ation of someone's imagination. They are a concept, a legal entity, and very hard for the average person to define accurately. That's all the more reason for the vision to be made as concrete, clear, com-pelling, and visceral as possible. If the vision can be visually depicted, all the better. Stories and examples help bring abstract concepts alive.

Consider a vision statement that reads: "Ajax aspires to be the preeminent manufacturer of O-rings in the world, to provide supe-rior customer service, and to be a preferred place of employment for its employees." While each word may have been carefully pon-dered by the executive group, the fact of the matter is that the name "Ajax" and the product "O-rings" could be replaced by hun-dreds of others and no one would notice.

Link the Vision to Each Team and Individual

With a clear vision statement in place, leaders can now discuss with each associate in the organization how her work connects with that vision. If that linkage is not readily apparent, this is a strong signal that either what the person is doing needs to be substantially redefined or that the leader needs to clarify how the individual's work is tied to the overall goals. You'd hope that this connection would be extremely obvious. If it isn't, then quick action should be taken.

Clarify What Path Not to Take

It has been noted that one of the most valuable outcomes of achieving greater strategic clarity is that it tells people what *not* to do as much as it tells them what *to* do. In many organizations, there is a belief that the more things we do, the better. While this is never stated overtly, the underlying mentality is:

> We will take on any and all customers that we can. We'll embark on any new project that someone is enthused about. We'll develop any new project or service in which a customer shows interest.

Clarity of vision helps all members of the group to be vigilant about not attempting to serve everyone who wants to be a customer, or to embark on any project about which someone becomes enthused, or to create a new product because one prospect or client expresses interest in it. These are hard decisions to make, especially for newly created organizations that are scratching out their existence. But given their limited resources, it is especially crucial for those companies to stay focused.

Ideally, as part of the vision, stating what is not included, what won't be undertaken, and what will be postponed until a future date is a valuable addition.

Align Systems with the Vision

Visions of the preferred future can easily be created, but they are then injected into an existing organization with its current systems, policies, procedures, and behavioral norms. It is very unreasonable to believe that the new vision will survive in an environment that was not created to sustain it.

> Our own organization is a good case in point. The decision was made to move from being primarily a consulting organization to an organization that was more focused on defined products and solutions. While there was agreement among all the executives that this was the correct "go-forward" strategy, the implications of this simple decision were enormous. This decision required new systems and procedures for product development and product management, new compensation systems, new customer support staff, new organizational functions and structure—indeed, the list seemed endless. But to have announced a new vision and not to have made those changes would have caused many people inside the organization to initially be puzzled and ultimately become disillusioned, because of the contradiction between what we were actually doing and what we said we wanted to do.

Consistently and Continually Communicate the Vision and Direction

Indeed, one of the interesting issues in creating a vision involves the need for its constant repetition by the leaders. Why? Don't people have memories that retain such ideas? They seem to remember thousands of other things that were said that have much less importance. Why do colleagues seem to forget the vision and strategy? The answer may be that they don't forget. They don't have amnesia. We suspect that the answer lies somewhere else.

The metaphor that comes to mind involves something that happens in many marriages or domestic partnerships. They begin with expressions of love between partners. Then, as daily events occur, things happen that erode the strength of that relationship, or at least raise questions about it. One party says or does things that seem contrary to that original expression of love as the other party sees it. Martin Seligman, in his book *Authentic Happiness*, points out that the most happily united couples spend a few minutes at the beginning of each day getting caught up, talking about their expectations for the day, reassuring each other of their love, giving a kiss good-bye, and parting in a pleasant manner. The same thing happens each evening. It is clear that the most happily joined partners provide each other with a continuous stream of reassurance of their commitment and fidelity to the partnership. We believe there's an important principle embedded here.

Why is it that leaders must constantly reaffirm the goals and direction? Because in the whirlwind of daily activities, things are said and done that appear at worst to contradict or at best to be disconnected from the avowed strategy.

> One of the authors worked for a multinational pharmaceutical company. The firm brought all division and country managers together twice a year to discuss overall corporate strategy and direction. At the conclusion of these meetings, everyone seemed completely clear about and at peace with the strategy and his role in making it happen. Then, after a month or so, the author would visit many of these other locations, and he observed a very consistent phenomenon. Invariably there would be questions of: "Where is this organization headed?" "Our division can't formulate our strategy until we get clear about where the corporation is going."

Again, we don't believe that these leaders, who were so competent and senior, suddenly experienced amnesia or minor memory lapses. Something else was going on, and we can only surmise that in the ongoing stream of communication that came from headquarters, those in the remote locations heard messages that contradicted or eroded what they had earlier been told.

Whatever the cause, the need for leaders to repeat the direction and vision for the organization frequently is extremely important. It simply cannot be done too frequently.

Devise Tactics with a Greater Assurance That They Will Mesh with the Vision and Strategy

Without a clear vision, there is a high likelihood that tactics won't be perfectly aligned. With a clear vision and a strategy that is frequently reiterated, there is a much higher likelihood that the operational tactics selected by everyone in the organization will be in harmony with the vision. Leaders need to pay special attention to the priorities that are established in the organization. Often, after a vision has been established in the organization, competing priorities start to become established that create confusion about the strategy. Team members struggle to know when they should do anything they can to please a customer and when they should tell a customer that the customer's request is outside the mission of the organization.

Implement the Bold Changes Required to Make the Vision Real

Many visions are never realized because, while leaders want to achieve a vision, they lack the ability or commitment to make difficult changes. Any new vision will require change, and change rarely occurs automatically because there is a new vision or by declaration. Change requires discipline to continue to make decisions and take actions that are consistent with a desired outcome.

Remember That External Focus Is Critical

Leaders who are attempting to implement a new vision need to stay connected with and informed about what is happening outside the organization. Implementing a new vision can cause leaders to become internally focused. All their energy and attention is focused internally, within the organization. This is a very dangerous position because the world is changing, competition is adapting, and customers are fickle. Leaders need to spend a significant portion of their time focusing outside the organization to make themselves aware of new trends.

Plan for Any Potential Setbacks

Finally, we would strongly urge that leaders anticipate problems. Some become so enamored with their new vision that they assume it will automatically be implemented. This never happens. There are always roadblocks and problems. Leaders need to take the time up front to anticipate these problems. That way, potential solutions are much more likely to be found, and successful implementations for their visions can be created.

EXAMPLES OF THE POWER OF VISION
Rethinking the Fundamental Product or Service That You Provide

A CEO of a large telecommunication company addresses 50 executives and indicates that while the old legacy company used to sell communication services, the new company has become part of the fabric of society. The live evidence of this in his home is that his children use their cell phones as alarm clocks. Indeed, the evolution of the cell phone's role in people's lives is hard to fully comprehend. It has become a primary means of communication, as young people text-message each other when they are less than 100 feet apart. The phone has become the primary camera to capture and send visual images. It is an entertainment device in downtime periods. It is the most often used calculator. It replaces the laptop computer for the business traveler with its ability to retrieve e-mail, spreadsheets, and lengthy documents.

Vision Creates Unifying Targets

A CEO of an energy company that five years before was teetering on the edge of bankruptcy now has a vision of making his company one of the best companies to work for in the world.

Not being satisfied with merely above-average employee satisfaction, the CEO describes his vision for moving the company into the top quartile.

Vision Helps to Implement an Important Strategic Initiative

A human resources executive has a vision of developing leaders that are world class in terms of their skills and competencies. This organization had done little to develop leaders in the past. It has definite financial constraints on what it can spend for this activity. The executive buys books and distributes them to critical stake-holders in the organization. She has "lunch and learn" discussions to share her vision and build support. She arranges special meetings with a few executives who show some interest and talks them into having a pilot program. She attends every pilot and follows up with each participant. Within a year, 200 leaders have been through a meaningful developmental experience. The organization is making progress in helping people to acquire critical skills that will enable them to take on bigger roles in the company.

These are just a few examples of leaders with a clear vision who inspire their organizations to new levels of performance and improvement.

CONCLUSION

1. Begin a process that will create a clear vision and direction for the organization. Involve your team. This is not a solo flight.
2. Combine the organization's guiding principles with the picture of what the organization wants to be in a few years. The vision should capture the important guiding principles and values. Can you make a graphic representation of the vision?
3. Establish a clear line of sight between each individual's work and where the organization wants to go.
   - Discuss with each individual how his work connects with the vision.
   - Redefine to each person what he *should* be doing or clarify how his work connects to the overall goals.
4. Identify what is trivial to achieving the vision of the organization and what is titanic. Make sure that people know what *not*

to do. Ask the question, "Are we taking on more than we can handle?"

5. Align systems and initiatives around the vision. Explore whether the new vision will survive in a system that was not specifically designed to sustain it.

6. Regularly communicate the vision and direction. Provide a continuous stream of reassurance to others. Devise tactics that mesh with the vision and the strategy.

7. For additional information and resources on this topic, go to www.zengerfolkman.com and click on the Inspiring Leader icon.

Chapter 9

Communicating Powerfully

The new source of power is not money in the hands of a few, but information in the hands of many.

—John Naisbitt

Put it before them briefly so they will read it, clearly so they will appreciate it, picturesquely so they will remember it and above all accurately so they will be guided by its light.

—Joseph Pulitzer

It will surprise no one that communicating powerfully is one of the behaviors linked to a leader's ability to inspire. If we think "inspirational leader," most of us would immediately think "terrific communicator." While there is clearly an extremely high level of correlation between communication and inspiration, the two are not synonymous. For example, we found leaders who were seen as highly effective communicators, but who were not perceived as being highly inspirational. Something sets the highly inspirational leaders apart from those who are not, and it isn't simply that they are good communicators. After analyzing our data, we think it can be summarized in the following elements.

A DOZEN KEYS TO INSPIRING COMMUNICATION
Seek Opportunities to Communicate

Inspiring leaders think about communication in a different way. They never see it as a chore. On the contrary, they welcome opportunities to communicate. They don't turn down chances to talk at a leadership development seminar or at a meeting of the company's internal auditors. There are no bad opportunities to communicate if a group of company employees is assembled and if the event can possibly fit into their schedule.

Communication is not just a process by which leaders do their job; they see it *as* their job. It is a different mindset from the one held by the leader who dribbles out information reluctantly, on a "need-to-know" basis.

We earlier wrote about Andy Pearson, the chairman of Yum, who made such a remarkable turnabout in his own leadership style. David Dorsey wrote about that transformation in his communication practices:

> Pearson's new leadership style is more than a way of relating to people. It involves the nuts and bolts of what he does from day to day, the processes that define the company's operations. Where before, Pearson would have dealt with only a small team of direct reports, he now seeks contact with people at all levels. It's his responsibility to motivate people across the company. He now believes that it's less important to issue orders than it is to seek answers and ideas from below. His job is to listen to the people who work for him and to serve them.
>
> "My old mantra was to influence the direction and behavior of a relatively small circle of direct reports," Pearson said. Now he and Novak move their values and ideas across the organization through programs such as CHAMPS, which rewards employees for recognizing the best practices of fellow workers, and through regular visits to the restaurants, during which they study those practices and reward people for good work.[1]

The transformation just described is huge. The recipients of Pearson's communication changed from a small circle of direct reports to people at all levels of a behemoth organization. It also changed from infrequent contact with that inner circle to a relentless pattern of visiting restaurants all over the world to connect constantly with employees.

Expand the Volume and Frequency

Andy Pearson illustrates this second element of the inspiring communicator. As noted earlier, widening the circle of people with whom you communicate and multiplying the frequency of meeting with front-line employees represents a complete reversal of thinking about how senior leaders communicate within a giant organization. We still encounter a few leaders who hold to the old notion that communication should be on a need-to-know basis. The information that this person shares with subordinates and peers is driven solely by what these potential recipients require in order to perform their jobs.

> In our consulting work, we meet these people. They are alive and well in many organizations. While their numbers appear to be in sharp decline, they see information as having value only if a person has an immediate need to use it. These "need-to-know" and "keep it close to your vest" communicators fear that information will leak to the wrong people or clutter the thinking of the person who doesn't really need it.
>
> This position is becoming increasingly hard to maintain in a world where so many have access to the Internet, which makes such vast amounts of information instantly available to everyone. Company chat boards have come to mean that few things are either sacred or secret. This democratization of information is in sharp contrast to the tight hold on communication practiced by the old-school manager who sought to hoard it. There is not one shred of doubt about which of these philosophies will prevail in the long run. Information is simply going to be available in ever-increasing amounts and with ever-quickening speed. Those who seek to hoard information

are fighting a losing battle and are completely out of synch with the world about them.

But this perspective has a seductive logic to it. Why take the time to communicate information that someone doesn't absolutely need? Isn't that wasteful of both parties' time? Doesn't it encumber others with data that really aren't all that useful to them? Aren't there risks in having information circulating among employees that could find its way to competitors?

The counter to all of these concerns and arguments is that communication is not primarily a logical issue. There is an extremely important psychological element to it that completely swamps the logical dimension. Providing people with information that is meaningful to them is far more than a simple cognitive interaction in which some fact or opinion is passed from you to me.

The communication process involves the exchange of some information, ideas, or perceptions. The process of making that exchange creates a relationship between the parties. This interaction and relationship are often far more important than the piece of information that was passed between the two people.

The level of people's commitment and engagement is affected by how they are treated, and one of the key elements of that treatment is driven by the information they receive. People may not _need_ to know, but they desire to know. Knowing gives them a feeling of membership or inclusion in the organization. They feel trusted. Rather than "sitting at the children's table," they feel like adult members of the family. If an organization wants to create unity and cohesion in its culture, then it must share information more widely.

Furthermore, the person withholding information may seriously misjudge when some information will be extremely important for a subordinate to understand. It isn't always possible to foresee the emergencies or events that could arise that would require this subordinate to use this information. Can people be too well informed?

Max DePree, the former CEO of Herman Miller, was an astute student of leadership. DePree talked of the need for "lavish communication." In contrast to the mentality that would communicate only on a need-to-know basis, DePree routinely communicated to the entire workforce about a number of important topics, including the following:

1. Extensive financial information
2. Productivity measures
3. The status of new products under development
4. Competitive information
5. Customer satisfaction measures
6. Quality statistics
7. Review of the corporate strategy
8. Refresher on the mission, vision, and values of the organization.

We applaud the concept of lavish communication. Imagine the impact that this has on the level of engagement and commitment of all employees. Every employee is now in a position to make smarter decisions whenever important issues arise. Beyond that, being trusted with that information, and having upper management take the time to communicate so extensively, clearly signals the importance of the front-line associates of the firm.

Go for the Big Issues

The inspiring leader doesn't shy away from important issues. In fact, the evidence is that such leaders prefer to move upstream to the bigger or thornier issues. If rumors of a reorganization are flying around, the inspiring leader is inclined to step right into it, asking what people are hearing, inquiring about the concerns they have, and then telling the listeners everything that is appropriate to be passed on.

Some topics are trivial and others are titanic. The more important the topic, the more attention and concern will be paid to it by those in attendance. Our experience has been that when leaders successfully convey that all topics are fair game for discussion, that leader's influence goes up.

> In a group meeting, someone asks, "Why did Al Hartman leave the company?"
>
> Answer: "In this case, for some legal reasons, I'm sorry I can't tell you everything I know. But I can say that he was frustrated with me and didn't agree with some decisions I made that affected him. I'm sorry to see him leave. Things will get back to normal in a couple of weeks, but in no way was he pushed out."
>
> That answer is much better than, "We can't talk about it." (Candor builds trust and is inspirational to the listeners.)

Keep It Positive

An extensive body of literature demonstrates the importance of communication being positive and uplifting, rather than being negative. Two researchers observed 60 leadership teams who were performing their annual strategic planning, problem-solving, and budgeting activities. These researchers were investigating why some teams performed better than others. Their startling discovery was that the one factor that was twice as powerful as anything else in predicting the teams' success was the ratio of positive comments (approval, suggestions, praise, appreciation, compliments, and overall support) to negative comments (pointing out faults, disparagement, criticism, or disapproval). The ratio of positive to negative comments in the highest-performing teams was 5 to 1, in medium-performing teams it was just below 2 to 1, and in the low-performing teams it was roughly 1 positive for every 3 negative.[2] Studies done in both industry and marriage counseling reinforce the value of positive communication outnumbering any kind of negative messages by roughly 5 to 1.[3] Organizations that achieve this ratio are far more apt to perform at an extremely high level.

There are times and places when more critical messages must be delivered, but that clearly works best if there has been a preponderance of positive messages preceding the negative ones.

Ask More Questions; Give Fewer Orders

Similarly, it has been shown that there is an optimum ratio of declarative or instructional messages to a leader's asking questions. In high-performing organizations, the ratio of questions to instructions is slightly higher than 1 to 1, whereas in low-performing organizations, the ratio is more on the order of 20 instructions to every question asked.[4]

Share the Spotlight

The leaders in high-performing organizations had roughly the same number of comments that were about others as that were about themselves. That equality in focus was in sharp contrast to low-performing organizations, in which leaders made 33 times more comments about themselves than they did about others in the organization. The behavior that conveys, "It's all about me" reduces the level of motivation and commitment of others.[5]

Step into the Listeners' Shoes

The inspiring leader thinks about the listeners. There are many ways to approach presenting any issue or topic. If there's a new product being developed, the leader could talk about how it was conceived and the breathtaking advantages of this new technology compared to the old ways. But the inspiring leader adds one more ingredient: WIIFM—"What's in it for me?" The leader recognizes that many listeners will be thinking, "Will this new product be manufactured somewhere else? Will it cause the company to shrink or to grow?" So whether it is a new product, a rumored merger, a reorganization, the installation of a new enterprise software program, or a sudden decline in the stock price, the inspiring leader always connects the event to the listener and does everything possible to convey as honest and as upbeat a message as possible.

> Stu Reed, the executive vice president of integrated supply chain management for Motorola, was the 2007 recipient of Communications World's EXCEL Award. Reed noted that public relations professionals often work hard to create two paragraphs of eloquent prose, but when he looked at the essence of what they meant to say, it boiled down to a simple message, such as "Hang in there; times are tough." Reed's philosophy is to communicate with simple messages. He believes that people "pick up passion more than eloquence." Reed consistently frames his messages in the form of stories that others can repeat. Finally, Reed ends every message by attempting to connect the problem or issue with the individual. So the ending of every conversation or presentation comes down to "What does it mean to you?"

Make It Two-Way

Inspiring communication is not just one-way, but more often a two-way transaction. Our emphasis is often on the sending or producing side of the equation. The need for the communicator to be the receiver or collector of messages can be easily overlooked.

Think again about the chairman of Yum, Andy Pearson, visiting a Taco Bell restaurant and talking with the front-line employees. He asks them questions about the best practices they've been observing on the part of their fellow workers. He listens and takes notes. This is two-way communication at its best.

> For centuries, we have attempted communication "downward." This, however, cannot work, no matter how hard and how intelligently we try. It cannot work, first, because it focuses on what we want to say. It assumes, in other words, that the utterer communicates. There can be no communication if it is conceived as going from

"I" to "thou." Communication works only from one
member of "us" to "another."

—Peter Drucker

Use Multiple Communication Techniques and Opportunities

Great communicators are seldom "one-celled." They use a broad
spectrum of techniques and find a wide variety of occasions to communicate. Here's a quick review of some:

- *One-on-one dialogue.* Communication is often between individuals of whom one has power or position. The key to this communication is that it be candid and direct. By its very nature, it
  should also be personal. Messages should be crafted with the
  uniqueness of the individual in mind. The most effective one-on-
  one communicators have the ability to focus all their attention
  and energy on connecting with this one person. These interactions allow both parties to carefully observe facial expressions and
  body language, along with the words that are said.

  Individuals are inspired in their one-on-one interactions with
  their leader. The leader who uses every meeting as a chance to
  inspire is taking advantage of golden opportunities.

- *Attendee at a meeting.* Let's assume that you've gone to a meeting where you are a participant. You are not in charge. Effective
  leaders inject their opinion in meetings, make proposals for how
  to move forward, and in general are perceived as making
  thoughtful comments. They don't just sit in any meeting, acting
  aloof and uninvolved because they are not running the meeting.
  They are comfortable with challenging ideas and bringing
  extremely different points of view to the surface. They help
  people analyze their own assumptions about an issue.[6] They are
  not contentious and disruptive. Constructive behavior in meetings is a key element of inspiring and motivating others.

- *Conducting meetings.* Leaders are in a position to organize and
  conduct many meetings. Each is an excellent opportunity to communicate important messages. There's a big difference, however,

between being in charge and being a smothering leader. When they are "in charge," inspiring leaders refrain from dominating the conversation. They encourage ideas to come from others in the group, rather than being the one who always provides them. The best leaders never speak first on a complex topic unless it is simply to frame the issue. If the leader goes beyond that to express a strong point of view, that most often has a chilling effect on others speaking up and saying what they truly believe. By holding back and speaking at the end, the leader encourages others to speak. They then say what they truly believe. This avoids the frequent posturing that sometimes occurs that is primarily geared toward gaining the approval of the leader.

> Charisma becomes the undoing of leaders. It makes them inflexible, convinced of their own infallibility, and unable to change.
>
> —Peter Drucker

While Drucker's comment focuses only on the negative dimension of charisma, this is an extremely interesting observation about leadership. As you would suppose, we don't agree. There are leaders who are extremely charming and forceful. Their dominant personalities sway people to accept their opinions. Others are intimidated. No one stands up to or challenges the point of view of this powerful leader. We wouldn't describe this person as truly inspiring, especially in the long run.

As Drucker pointed out, the charisma of leaders can become their undoing. Becoming convinced of their own infallibility puts leaders on a course in which they believes themselves to be above the rules that others must play by. Such isolation from the opinion and feedback of others leads to egregious behavior. But Drucker is presumably talking about an extreme case of someone relying on one or two charismatic qualities while forgetting what makes the well-rounded, truly inspiring leader.

One very useful tactic for improving the communication in meetings is for leaders to ask probing questions that convey the expectation that all individuals have the opportunity (and, to some degree, the responsibility if they have a different opinion from those already expressed) to weigh in on every question before they state their personal view.

- *Presentations.* Another communication process involves making presentations. While we will argue that this is only one of several dimensions of being a good communicator, there is no question that the ability to make well-organized, dynamic presentations in front of employee groups, customers, and other stakeholders is an important communication skill. It is a moment that can be extremely inspirational.

  We have colleagues who teach presentation skills to leaders. Often a leader's career is frozen because of a lack of polish in making presentations, or because the leader is terribly awkward in public settings. These colleagues report that following a relatively short period of training on presentation skills and some coaching on ways to improve her "presence," promotions often follow. While this evidence is clearly anecdotal, it provides some confirmation that poor presentation skills, because they are so public, often hold people back in their career.

  The content of presentations needs to be well thought through. What's said must be interesting, relevant, and organized in a way that the listeners can comprehend. We recommend a book by Barbara Minto, *The Pyramid Principle: Logic in Writing, Thinking, and Problem Solving,* that is available directly from the author. For decades she trained McKinsey & Co. consultants to write and create compelling proposals, reports, and presentations. Her format for creating presentations and organizing reports is practical.

  The best communicators, according to our research, are adept at tailoring the message to their listeners. That doesn't mean that the story completely changes based on who the audience is. It simply means that the speaker is aware of the interests and concerns of those in the audience, and that the presentation is crafted to respond to those needs and interests. The speaker begins the preparation of the presentation by pondering: "What does this mean to my audience?" "Why should people be concerned?" "What will be seen as negative or positive in my message?" "What questions will immediately be raised?"

Tell Relevant Stories

One remarkable communication technique is to tell stories. (*Stories* is a word with multiple meanings. We obviously mean true stories.) Maybe this is a holdover from our childhood experience, but stories are both riveting and memorable. There is something about the narrative form and the specificity that draws people into the event. Stories become even better if there is some emotion injected into the story. When there is emotion, the story becomes a giant magnet that draws people's attention and leads them to ignore many distractions. For every major point the speaker is trying to make, there should be a good story that illustrates that point. This has the double effect of creating greater clarity about the message and making it stick in the listener's memory.

Inspiring presenters in public forums have learned a simple lesson: reading text is just plain boring. Telling stories transforms the presentation and breathes life into it. Humor and personal anecdotes spice it up. A presentation style that has enthusiasm and wraps major ideas in some emotion makes the presentation "zing." For additional information on how leaders can communicate in a way that inspires and motivates others, please visit our Web site at www.zengerfolkman.com and click on the Inspiring Leader icon.

Keep the Pace Brisk

Today's audiences are accustomed to fast-paced presentations. If you watch a movie that is a few decades old, you are struck by its slow pace. Scenes change every two to three minutes, whereas in modern cinema, changes occur every few seconds.

Communicate Passion and Enthusiasm

The most effective performers, as a rule, are those who throw themselves into the performance. The performer who is placid, calm, and sedate seldom captures the audience as much as the person who performs with intensity and passion. The same principles apply to the leader as communicator. The listeners hear the words, but they respond equally as much to the passion and emotion.

> At a large conference attended by delegates from all over the world, an executive was speaking. One person at a back table turned to his neighbor and remarked, "I can't understand one word he's saying, he's got such a strong accent. But it doesn't matter. You can tell how excited he is about where we're headed. It's obvious he believes it. That's all I need to hear."

Shakespeare wrote *Henry V* nearly 200 years after the Battle of Agincourt (1415). Many feel that it is the finest dramatic interpretation of what leadership meant in the Middle Ages. It was a deeply emotional message that served to lift the soldiers' spirits to the highest level to prepare them for a battle in which they were seriously outnumbered.

Henry had ordered his army to advance and to start a battle that, given the state of his army, he would have preferred to avoid. The English had very little food, had marched 260 miles in 2½ weeks, were suffering from sickness (such as dysentery), and faced much larger numbers of well-equipped French men-at-arms. However, Henry needed to get to the safety of Calais, and he knew that if he waited, the French would get more reinforcements. While estimates regarding the size of each army vary widely, the most common conclusion is that the French outnumbered the English 3 to 1.

The French suffered a catastrophic defeat, not only in terms of the sheer numbers killed, but also because of the number of high-ranking nobles they lost.

One fairly widely used estimate puts the English casualties at 450, which is not an insignificant number to lose out of an army of 6,000, but far less than the 10,000 the French lost. It was one of the greatest victories of England over France in all their combined history.

Prior to the battle, the morale in the English line must have been extremely low. King Henry, rising to the occasion, spoke words of encouragement that rallied the English troops and carried them to a victory.

The speech given here is fictional. There was no scribe there to transcribe it. It is believed, however, that Shakespeare had some accounts from those who had been there. It illustrates how strong medieval kings ruled through the strength of their convictions and by force of their personality.

(Just for fun, if your circumstances allow it, read this speech aloud. Do it as if you were a great Shakespearean actor, with all the feeling you can muster.)

St. Crispen's Day Speech

Excerpts from *Henry V*, by William Shakespeare, 1599. (The full text of this speech from the play is in Appendix 3.)

Enter the King

Westmoreland: O, that we had here
But one ten thousand of those men in England
That do no work today.
King King Henry V: What's he that wishes so?
My cousin Westmoreland? No, my fair cousin.
If we are marked to die, we are enow

To do our country loss, and if to live,
The fewer men, the greater share of honor.
God's will! I pray thee wish not one man more.
...
Rather proclaim it, Westmoreland, through my host
That he which hath no stomach to this fight,
Let him depart. His passport shall be made
And crowns for convoy put into his purse.
We would not die in that man's company
That fears his fellowship to die with us.
This day is called the feast of Crispian.
He that outlives this day and comes safe home
Will stand a-tiptoe when this day is named,
And rouse him at the name of Crispian.
...
This story shall the good man teach his son.
And Crispin Crispian shall ne'er go by
From this day to the ending of the world,
But we in it shall be remembered—
We few, we happy few, we band of brothers.
For he today that sheds his blood with me
Shall be my brother....
And gentlemen in England now abed
Shall think themselves accursed they were not here,
And hold their manhoods cheap whiles any speaks
That fought with us upon Saint Crispin's Day.

When some people think of leadership behavior that inspires and motivates, they think of speeches such as this one delivered by King Henry V. This is an ultimate example of a leader's ability to inspire troops to willingly go onto the battlefield when they realize that there is a high likelihood that they might die. It is a classic example of important messages being surrounded with powerful emotion.

Note how Henry steps into the most pressing, visceral issue facing his men. They were outnumbered. Rather than shying away from the issue, he hits it head on. He then makes this obvious disadvantage into an advantage by essentially saying, "We'll have fewer people with whom to share our glory." Henry invites anyone "which hath no stomach to this fight" to leave, arguing that no hero would want to die in that man's company.

Part of the speech's power comes from the words that Shakespeare chose to have King Henry speak. Survivors will "stand a-tiptoe when this day is named." And then comes the ultimate emotional plea in King Henry's final argument that men of England who aren't there with them "shall think themselves accursed" and "hold their manhoods cheap whiles any speaks that fought with us upon Saint Crispin's Day."

Inspirational talks have their place. However, one highly encouraging outcome of our research is our conclusion that it isn't only impassioned speeches, such as this one, that characterize the most effective leaders' inspirational quality. This is but one of many vehicles that can be used to inspire. Such leaders do a number of things that excite their colleagues to peak performance.

A team of researchers has written about the role of senior leadership teams. These researchers write:

> What does it take for a chief executive to inspire a leadership team with a vision, to get members to focus intently and passionately on what is special about the enterprise? One popular image is that of a leader on a podium, revving up the troops with a rousing talk. That can help, and if you are an inspirational speaker, you should, of course, take the pulpit whenever you have the chance. But what if you are neither comfortable nor particularly effective in giving talks that bring people to their feet? There are many other ways to inspire.[7]

They recount an experience with Don Burr, founder of People Express Airline. "Nothing is more important than charismatic leadership," he had explained to his team, "and if you doubt it look at what Mike does with his team."

Burr's comment took everyone aback because Mike was rather shy and normally quiet. Burr proceeded, "Mike doesn't stand up and make long speeches like I do, but his understanding of our precepts and his deep commitment to our customers shines through in everything he says and does. He has his own special kind of charisma. And that's what I expect of you, to use your special gifts, whatever they may be, to inspire others to share your vision for our company."

The authors conclude, "Inspirational leadership is indeed an essential competence for the leaders of senior teams. But there is no one best way to provide it. The key is to identify which of your skills and styles can best be used to create in others the passion you feel for your work and then to hone and develop those resources as one core element in your personal repertoire of team leadership skills."[8]

STEPS TO TAKE

1. Make a conscious decision about the general philosophy or policy that you will follow with regard to communication. When? Who else must be involved?
2. Review the communication pattern you have with your direct reports. How often do you have one-on-one meetings with them? How would you describe the quality of those meetings? How could they be improved?
3. Next, review the communication you have with your peers. How often do you meet with your peers? How would you describe the nature of those communications? How could they be improved?
4. Reflect on your participation in meetings. In meetings that you don't conduct, do you contribute frequently? Do you ask questions? Give opinions?
5. In meetings that you conduct, do you give your opinion last?
6. In meetings that you conduct, do you focus on the process of the meeting (making sure that there's a high level of participation, that the discussion doesn't get stuck, and that everyone feels free to disagree)?

7. Rate your presentation skills. How do you compare to the best that you've experienced? What could you do to improve your presentations? Do you prepare well-organized messages? Are you skillful at tailoring messages to fit the audience? Is your delivery enthusiastic, warm, and with appropriate humor? Are you a skilled teller of stories that illustrate key points and make presentations highly interesting? Overall, how could you improve your presentations?

8. Think of some examples of your being an "antenna" for your work group. These are times when you bring information back to your group that you've obtained from reading, conversations with those outside the firm, participation in industry associations, and so on.

9. How diligent are you in passing on information that you collect to your colleagues?

Chapter 10

Developing People

The best executive is the one who has sense enough to pick good men to do what he wants done and self restraint to keep from meddling with them while they do it.
—Theodore Roosevelt

When team members think about the rewards they receive from their jobs, after the pay and benefits, the next most tangible reward is the learning and development that come from training, job assignments, and experiences at work. Leaders who create positive developmental experiences for their team members are much more apt to create an inspired and motivated team. Conversely, when team members see a job as just work, with no learning or development, then it is far more difficult for them to find their work inspirational.

One of the authors, while in graduate school, was a research assistant for a professor who every decade summarized the research from every journal in his specialty. The assigned task was to read every article and classify the research methods used. Hundreds of journal issues needed to be read and analyzed. On a rare occasion, an article would be of some interest to a young, naïve graduate student. But the majority of the time it was simply a boring and meaningless job. It took a great deal of discipline and fortitude just to walk to the library and begin reading every day. At the end of the semester, the student made a frantic effort to get an assignment with another professor. Grading statistics tests would have felt like a huge promotion. In this case there was no real learning, no development, and hence no inspiration— just drudgery.

But think of how exciting this assignment could have been had it been positioned and managed in a different way. In hindsight, the professor could have made it into a great developmental opportunity for a student. What a rare opportunity to be paid to read a decade's worth of literature in your field! Periodic discussions with the professor about interesting articles that had been reviewed would have made the project come to life. Merely understanding what the professor was actually seeking for his teaching and research purposes would have made a huge difference. If the student had known how the professor would use this information, it could have been a far more fruitful endeavor. Permission to dismiss articles that were peripheral to the professor's interests or treat them lightly would have made the student feel trusted and more of a colleague rather than a hired hand or servant and would have saved considerable time and wasted effort.

BENEFITS OF DEVELOPMENT

When people have opportunities for development, there are several personal benefits.

- They are more likely to stay employed by the organization.
- Their satisfaction with their job increases.
- They are more productive.
- They produce higher-quality work.

However, in addition to the individuals' personal satisfaction, there is a secondary payoff from the leader's having created a learning environment. Simply put, the organization keeps getting better, and people like to be associated with a winning organization. When the leader creates a climate of learning, the outcome is continual improvement on the part of the organization. Mistakes do not get repeated. Information that is held by one group is freely passed to others who can benefit from it. The dependency that the organization might have had on a few people is now shared more broadly. Why is development so inspiring?

GROWING AND DEVELOPING IS A FUNDAMENTAL HUMAN NEED

Dr. Maxwell Maltz wrote the book *Psycho-Cybernetics* at age 61, as the climax of an already varied, colorful, and exceptionally successful career. For many years, Dr. Maltz had a flourishing practice as a reconstructive and cosmetic facial surgeon, lectured internationally on his medical specialty, and pursued a dual career as a prolific author.

He moved from treating "outer scars" to "inner scars" after observing that many patients' unhappiness and insecurities were not cured, as they and he had believed they would be, when he gave them the perfect new faces they desired.

One of his metaphors from the book compared people to bicycle riders. "If they aren't moving forward, they fall over." That is a useful way to explain the importance of development. There is a powerful driving force inside most individuals that prods and pushes them to improve.

By our interpretation, roughly one-third of the strengths that were identified by Martin Seligman in his analysis of the signature strengths of individuals were strongly tied to the concept of improvement and moving forward.[1]

A FOCUS ON DEVELOPMENT EXPLAINS WHY PEOPLE SUCCEED

Carol Dweck, who teaches at Stanford University, has spent the last 30 years studying why some people succeed and others fail.[2] Her answers are surprising to many. It isn't about IQ points or other abilities that are bestowed on someone by an unseen hand. It has much more to do with their personal effort and application. And at the heart of it, she found that beginning at an early age, people begin to be divided into two camps. Which camp we're in explains how we become optimistic or pessimistic. It shapes our goals, our attitude toward work, and our relationships on the job. It affects our relationships with a spouse and how we raise our kids. It ultimately predicts whether or not we will fulfill our potential.

The first camp consists of those whose fundamental goal in life is to prove their worth to the people about them. They believe that their abilities are fixed, as if set in stone at an early age. And if you believe that your abilities are fixed at a high level, that means that you don't need to work hard. If your abilities happen to be fixed at a low level, then you are destined to failure, and working hard would not change anything. In either case, you have to repeatedly prove yourself. Your goal in life is to avoid serious challenges and escape experiencing failure that will show up the deficiencies that you've tried to keep hidden. This is the path of stagnation.

The second group is made up of those whose fundamental goal in life is to improve. For them, life is made up of a series of opportunities to be exploited and challenges to be overcome. This growth mindset is one in which you see yourself as fluid, a work in progress. You seek growth and opportunity. These people believe that talent is built over time and comes as the consequence of hard work and effort. Clearly the most successful people are those who fall into the "improving" category. Dweck reveals how high achievers in all fields—music, science, education, literature, sports, and business—apply the growth mindset to achieve results.

LEADERS CREATE MINDSETS

The encouraging news, however, is that mindsets can be changed. People can move from believing that their capabilities were fixed at an early age and can come to believe that "smart is something you get" and that people can actually progress throughout most of the course of their life.

Dweck's research shows that parents are a powerful force in shaping the mindset of a child. While her research focused on how parents and teachers influenced young children in their developmental stages, we are quite certain that how leaders in business treat their subordinates can have a similar, profound impact on how people view themselves on these two dimensions. The right kind of leadership helps people move from a "fixed" or "proving" mindset to one of "growth" and "improving." Exactly how the leader can be of greatest help to others will be described later in this chapter.

Research on the brain's ability to develop new neural networks is currently taking place at several research institutions and serves to confirm Dweck's fundamental thesis.

For example, in 1999, Princeton University released a stunning announcement regarding a reversal of a long-held theory that the capacity of the brain was fixed at birth. The headlines read: "Scientists Discover Addition of New Brain Cells in Highest Brain Area: Finding reverses long-held beliefs and has implications for designing therapies." The article went on to explain that this discovery confirmed that new neurons are being continually added to the cerebral cortex of adult monkeys and then explained that this reverses a strongly held belief that had existed for the last 100 years to the effect that the number of brain cells in primates was established at birth and that a certain number died each year through the adult years. This had strong implications for humans, because humans and monkeys have essentially the same brain structures.

This view that humans were born with a certain number of brain cells and that as we aged, a certain number of these cells died each year was in virtually every textbook on psychology published before 2000. This meant that mentally we were coasting on a long glide path through life, but always descending. Now the consensus among human brain researchers is that not only is the brain adding new cells, but at the same time new connections between brain cells are being made.

Questions to Ask Yourself

There clearly are some things that the leader must think and feel in order to be effective at developing subordinates, and thus be more inspirational and motivational.

1. *Do you possess a true concern for the development of others?* This genuine desire to see others get better is the first quality that is an absolute necessity. As most people begin their career, their focus is basically on their own success and making their mark in the organization. Once people have demonstrated their own capabilities, a number of them develop the desire to help other people make their mark.

2. *Are you deeply committed to helping others succeed?* This question is obviously related to the previous one. Rejoicing at the success of others requires a maturity and selflessness that is not always found in leaders who are clawing their way up the corporate ladder and who view other capable people as threats. Effective leaders are ones who make the transition from being concerned primarily about themselves and personal advancement to putting the team before self.

3. *Are continual improvement and learning personally important to you?* This obviously argues that the best leaders are part of the "growth" and "improving" category in Dweck's terminology. It is virtually impossible to be a great leader if you are in the camp of "proving" and "fixed abilities."

Some leaders believe that one of their prime opportunities and responsibilities is to help people learn. They willingly carve out time for people to attend relevant seminars and engage in activities that help to develop them. They budget generously for external development activities. They take time in staff meetings to discuss what was learned from each major project. These discussions often take the form of "after action reviews" that cover what had been intended to happen, what actually transpired, what caused the difference, and what should happen in the future for such events.

These three questions do not identify action steps that a leader can just arbitrarily take. They are visceral and bone-deep convictions and attitudes about people and their worth to the organization. The action steps being proposed next, however, work best when the three conditions above are solidly in place.

WHAT THE INSPIRATIONAL LEADER DOES TO DEVELOP OTHERS

Our research revealed some specific actions that leaders engaged in to develop subordinates.

Gives Coaching

An enormous amount has been written on coaching, its value to the individual, and its payoff for the organization. Dweck's research provides some insightful tips about the best approach to coaching. By translating Dweck's research on younger people to adult employees in a firm, you get some valuable suggestions.

Guy Kawasaki, the former McKinsey consultant and marketing guru, wrote about Dweck's research in a personal blog.[3] Here are his conclusions, and it is interesting to note that he has intuitively made the translation from how these principles apply to children to how they apply to employees:

> You have a bright child [employee], and you want her to succeed. You should tell her how smart she is, right?
>
> That's what 85 percent of the parents Dweck surveyed said. Her research on fifth graders shows otherwise. Labels, even though positive, can be harmful. They may instill a fixed mind-set and all the baggage that goes with it, from performance anxiety to a tendency to give up quickly. Well-meaning words can sap children's [employee's] motivation and enjoyment of learning and undermine their performance. While Dweck's study focused on intelligence praise, she says her conclusions hold true for all talents and abilities.

Here are Dweck's tips from Mindset:

- Listen to what you say to your kids [employees], with an ear toward the messages you're sending about mind-set.
- Instead of praising children's [employees'] intelligence or talent, focus on the processes they used.
  - Example: "That homework was so long and involved. I really admire the way you concentrated and finished it."
  - Example: "That picture has so many beautiful colors. Tell me about them."
  - Example: "You put so much thought into that essay. It really makes me think about Shakespeare in a new way."
- When your child [employee] messes up, give constructive criticism—feedback that helps the child [employee] understand how to fix the problem, rather than labeling or excusing the child [employee].
- Pay attention to the goals you set for your children [employees]; having innate talent is not a goal, but expanding skills and knowledge is.

Provides Actionable Feedback

Lots of people give advice. Managers frequently give advice to their subordinates. They, in turn, receive advice from various gurus who write books and give seminars based on only their opinions. But advice can be treacherous when it is either incorrect or not actionable. Often it is incorrect, especially if the person giving it didn't really understand the situation. The other problem, however, is that advice can simply be impossible to implement.

Part of that difficulty often comes from the general nature of the advice. We are reminded of the observation of Professor Karl Weick of the University of Michigan, in which he noted that any piece of advice could be two of three things, but could never be all three. The three things were as follows:

1. General
2. Simple
3. Accurate

Pick up any popular book on the subject of leadership. Randomly open it to some chapter that gives advice on a particular topic. Chances are that whatever the principle being professed, there are exceptions to it. In fact, you can often find two opposing points of view that have generally gained wide acceptance. This is why, while we respect the opinions of so many authors and leaders, we choose to focus on areas where we can provide evidence that is quantifiable, objective, and empirical as it relates to leadership.

As children, our parents often passed on proverbs that had been taught to them by their parents. The amusing fact is that virtually every proverb has a counterpart that contradicts it. Yet, when asked about each proverb separately, most people will indicate that they believe both to be true. Examples of this strange phenomenon include the following:

- Time waits for no man.
- Rome wasn't built in a day.

- A stitch in time saves nine.
- If it ain't broke, don't fix it.

- He who hesitates is lost.
- Look before you leap.

- The only constant is change.
- Order follows regulation.

- If at first you don't succeed, try, try again.
- Don't beat your head against a stone wall.

- Hitch your wagon to a star.
- The grass is always greener on the other side.

- The wish is father of the deed.
- If wishes were horses, beggars would ride.

- Life is what you make it.
- What will be, will be.

- Winning isn't everything; it's the only thing.
- Quit while you're ahead.

- Where there's a will, there's a way.
- You can't fit a round peg into a square hole.

- Paddle your own canoe.
- Two heads are better than one.

- Too many cooks spoil the broth.
- Many hands make light work.

- Ultimately there is but one truth.
- There are two sides to every story.

- Establish the rule and allow no variation.
- There is an exception to every rule.

Because much advice that is published or given in large seminars is by definition general and simple, it becomes obvious that it can't be accurate. Chris Argyris thinks that most of it doesn't work because it has too many "abstract claims, inconsistencies, and logical gaps to be useful as a concrete basis for concrete actions in concrete settings."[4] Argyris contends that no matter what managers hear from consultants, they ultimately resort to five behaviors. These are humorously described in the following terms:

1. State a message that's inconsistent ("You're in charge of this, but check in with Steve").
2. Act as if it's not inconsistent.
3. Make the inconsistency undiscussable.
4. Make the undiscussability undiscussable.
5. Act as if you're not doing any of the above.

Argyris argues that a choice is sound when it emphasizes facts and accumulated data and isn't influenced by the role, power, or positions of the people involved.

Argyris's advice on how to rectify this problem is to do the following:

- Specify the sequence of behavior required to produce an outcome. The more specific this is, the more likely it is that the advice will be successfully implemented.
- Define causality and make it exceedingly transparent (what causes us to get certain effects). Help the receiver to understand why what you are proposing is going to work. These are the steps of classic "behavior modeling" in which the facilitator provides either a live or videotaped example for the learner to watch, with a clear explanation of the key points being demonstrated and why they were important.
- Causality embedded in advice is testable in normal situations. Therefore, allow the person to test the advice being received. Suggest ways in which that test process can be conducted. What tests could easily be constructed to determine whether this advice was working?
- Specify the values or variables that govern the outcomes of the advice. What constitutes a good strategy, for example, may depend on whether the organization wants growth at all costs or

prefers risk avoidance. The recipient of advice needs to know the values that underlie the advice and also the outcomes that are being sought.

Argyris's suggestions take advice giving to a new level of sophistication.

Delegate in a Manner That Develops People

When tasks or projects are delegated to a subordinate, there is a seemingly infinite number of messages that can be conveyed. Here are a few of the messages that the recipient will listen for:

1. What the task consists of
2. Why the leader has delegated this task
3. Why the leader has chosen the person or group to whom the task or project is being given
4. What the leader conceives as the outcome
5. How the leader would like to be kept informed
6. The seriousness or consequences of the project or task

Clearly the leader can approach this delegation process with a strong task perspective and ignore the developmental implications. That is, the leader is concerned about the need to get something done on time, on budget, and with a minimal amount of turmoil being caused to the organization. Period. End of delegation discussion. The outcome, however, is that not much inspiration and motivation is likely to come from that conversation.

Let's assume that the leader sees the potential in this delegation conversation to provide a great deal of inspiration and motivation to the people receiving this project. Now the discussion on why the leader has delegated the task will take on a completely different character. The conversation could well include some dialogue like, "I see this project as a real opportunity to help you develop your skills in coordinating with the design group, operations, and marketing" or, "One of my reasons for delegating this to you is to prepare you to be able to handle much bigger projects on your own."

From there, the leader could say something like, "Sondra, I've chosen you for several reasons. I think you have the technical background to pull it off. You've demonstrated an extremely conscientious attitude about getting things done on time. I thought this would be a great developmental assignment. There are some others in the group who could probably pull it off successfully, but they wouldn't grow from the experience as much as I think you will." (Think about how Sondra is going to feel when she reflects on this conversation. Ponder the powerful and motivating messages that the leader has just conveyed. Some are overtly stated, but there are many messages that are "between the lines" and not spoken.)

But it doesn't need to end there. Now the leader continues the delegation dialogue by saying, "Here's what I envision to be the final deliverable that you and your team will produce. But I acknowledge that my conception is still a bit fuzzy. You'll have the opportunity to sharpen it. And the important point is that you'll have a strong voice in deciding how you get this all done. If you want to discuss with me how you plan to go about it, I'm available. That's your choice." (Again, sense the strong messages this leader has just sent and their motivational potential.)

Next the leader discusses the ideal way to be kept informed. "Sondra, because this project is so important and high profile, I feel some need to be kept abreast of your progress. Please understand that this is driven to a large extent by the people above me, but it's also because I'm very interested in knowing about your progress. How about us meeting once a week for the first month, and then maybe we should cut back to twice a month. All I want is your overall appraisal of progress against the milestones that you'll set in the project plan. If I can be of any help, please know that I'm available. The purpose of these meetings is not for me to insert myself or meddle; it's for me to be informed. I think one of my jobs is to provide 'air cover' for you and your team, and I can do that best if I'm knowledgeable about what's going on." (Again, the leader has conveyed some strong messages to Sondra that in most cases will have a profound motivational impact.)

In summary, the delegation process that is so familiar to leaders and carried out so frequently can occur in a perfunctory fashion. In that case, the motivational dimension of it will be minimal at best. Or, delegation can be elevated to an important discussion and can be wrapped with important messages that inspire and that generate positive motivation. It is all about how the leader elects to conduct the discussion.

Structure the Job with Development as the Objective

When a leader structures the job of each person in the group, there are many factors to consider. Clearly certain activities belong together. Many processes function best when they have one person overseeing the entire chain of activities. Effective leadership requires the person in charge to take many things into account when designing any job.

But when structuring a job, one dimension is often forgotten. One of the strongest drivers of motivation for any employee is the fundamental nature of the job itself. Precisely what does this person do during the working day? Expanding the employee's responsibilities usually increases the level of motivation. Providing greater variety (within some boundaries, obviously) usually also has that effect. Having the job expand in its breadth and depth will, in most cases, greatly expand the motivation of the person doing the job.

Frederick Herzberg, an early student of motivation in the workplace, came to the conclusion that the largest determinant of motivation for most people in organizations was directly proportional to the nature of the job itself. The huge mistake made by some of the leaders of the Industrial Revolution was to simplify jobs so that a person with a minimal amount of skill and experience could perform the work adequately. While there was a compelling logic that seemed to be driven by the economics of hiring less-skilled, lower-cost workers, there were huge unintended consequences. Dumbed-down jobs created apathetic workers who over time moved from not caring to ultimately becoming hostile toward management. Luckily, we have moved a long distance from many of those practices. However, insufficient attention is paid to the simple principle of making jobs challenging, responsible, with reasonable variety, and capable of helping people grow in the ways they desire.

Not every worker wants to grow and develop, but those who want that make remarkably greater contributions to their employers.

Make Developmental Experiences Available (Classes, Courses, Trips, Site Visits, and Benchmarking Opportunities)

One of the best organizations for excellent learning and development is the U.S. Marine Corps. A review of its recruits would reveal that the young men and women who entered the corps were of high quality, but they were not recruited from the elite universities and colleges of America. Most could not have gained admission to schools with extremely high admission standards. But after a few years, the same review would conclude that these individuals are now quite exceptional leaders. Their rigorous training has worked real magic. One aspect of their training experience that creates great value is that after every exercise, there is a debriefing activity in which decisions are discussed, alternative decisions are talked about, and feedback is provided. These are called "after action reviews."

Every business organization and public-sector agency has an enormous number of debriefing opportunities, but most of the time these organizations fail to sit down after a mission has ended, a decision has been made, or a project is concluded and debrief the experience. Such concrete reviews of actual events can be a much more meaningful learning experience than a class on how to conduct effective meetings, decision making, or project management.

The principle is simply that some of the best training opportunities are those that are directly linked to work issues. Leaders should take advantage of major on-the-job events and follow up with each of their employees regarding what was learned and how that learning can be applied in the future.

STEPS TO TAKE

1. Jot down the things you have done in the last month that sent a strong signal about your concern for the development of your team. If you can't think of any, then jot down what you could do in the coming month to accomplish that.

2. Schedule coaching times for the people on your team. Make yourself available to talk with each of them about performance questions and career progression and aspirations.

3. Think through how to delegate the next project to someone in your team in a way that emphasizes the developmental nature of it, as well as its other dimensions.

4. Review the way each person's job is structured to see if elements could be added that would be highly developmental.

5. Take seriously the creation of a development plan for each person on your team. Review it at least twice each year. Build in some rewards for following it and some consequences for ignoring it.

6. For additional free resources and information on how leaders develop people, go to www.zengerfolkman.com and click on the Inspiring Leader icon.

Chapter 11

Being Collaborative and a Good Team Player

The leaders who work most effectively, it seems to me, never say "I." And that's not because they have trained themselves not to say "I." They don't think "I." They think "we"; they think "team." They understand their job to be to make the team function. They accept responsibility and don't sidestep it, but "we" gets the credit. . . . This is what creates trust, what enables you to get the task done.

—Peter Drucker

Teams, not individuals, are the fundamental learning unit in modern organizations. This is where the "rubber stamp meets the road"; unless teams can learn, the organization cannot learn.

—Peter M. Senge

The most inspirational leaders are bone-deep team-oriented people, in contrast to those who are comfortable only in a traditional hierarchy, with its many layers and the shape of a steep pyramid. These leaders put the team before individuals. Inspirational leaders always talk of current and past success coming from the efforts of the team, not from the handiwork of any one person (especially themselves). When speaking of the future, these leaders invariably talk of the need for expanding collaboration and teamwork, realizing that future achievements will require extreme amounts of collaboration.

The importance of the mutual respect between a leader and the members of a team has an interesting history.

We're all familiar with the crowns worn by royalty. Some are bedecked with jewels set in elaborate gold and silver, with ornate filigree and elegant carving. So in ancient times, what crown might have been the one most treasured by its recipient? Could there be a crown considered to have far greater value than any creation of diamonds, sapphires, rubies, and gold?

What if we said that it was a crown made of grass? What's more, as hand-woven headpieces go, it wasn't particularly nice. It was not beautifully designed, and the weaving was rather crude. It was made of extremely simple materials and fashioned by the calloused hands of Roman legionnaires. But this Grass Crown was without question the most revered honor that any leader of that day could receive. Why?

It was not given by any single person. No king, emperor, or magistrate could confer it. Nor could any body such as a parliament or senate confer the Grass Crown. This was an award given by the soldiers to their general. It was always awarded by acclamation. The award was given in recognition of outstanding leadership that in a time of great crisis or trial enabled the army to be victorious.

The respect of one's subordinates is the ultimate tribute to an inspirational leader. As we have said before, if you want to know about the effectiveness of a leader, ask those who are led.

WHY IS A TEAM ORIENTATION SO EFFECTIVE IN INSPIRING PEOPLE TO HIGH PERFORMANCE?

It begins with the extreme complexity of most efforts in organizations. There are few tasks or projects in organizations today that can be completed by one person acting in isolation. The more important the task is, the more likely it is that it requires the cooperation of other departments to pull it off.

In Chapter 2, we noted the importance of productivity. Collaboration and teamwork utilize people to a greater degree. They engage people more fully. They take full advantage of people's intellect and passion as well as their willing hands.

Beyond that, from a front-line worker's perspective, nothing is more wasteful than to have artificial boundaries in the organization based on different leaders' definition of their turf. In ancient times, when princes were at odds with each other, but were conducting their covert personal battles in an overtly civil and dignified manner, the spear carriers who were loyal to each prince were on the battlefield killing each other. That phenomenon lives on inside modern organizations, where you see the subordinates of one executive working to outsmart and outflank their colleagues who report to another executive with whom their boss is at war. This is when statements like, "Don't talk to them," or "Don't give them anything that isn't absolutely necessary" get made. Sometimes this happens between competing divisions, such as Latin America versus Europe. Other times it happens between functional areas, such as when operations and sales are at odds with each other. Conflicts between the home office and the field are classic. In each case, it is the people at the lower levels who pay the high price.

NEGATIVE IMPACT OF HOSTILITY BETWEEN GROUPS

One of the most frustrating experiences that employees describe is being told by their boss that they are forbidden to cooperate with another group inside the company. In some cases, they are even forbidden to talk with the people from another department. For the employee who is attempting to serve a customer or complete a project on time and needs the help of those in another department, to then be told that such collaboration is off-limits is maddening and highly demotivating.

> We consulted with an organization that was a combination of two behemoth organizations that had joined forces to develop a new product jointly between them.

Their cultures were different. The assignments that people received were only temporary. Two leaders, one from each parent organization, were attempting to lead this project as "two-in-the-box" coleaders. One told the people with whom he had a close relationship that they must not talk to the people from the other company. The people at the lowest level recognized that the project's success absolutely depended on there being a close working relationship between the two groups, and they were caught in an uncomfortable vise. How do you resolve loyalty to your boss with your perceptions of what's good for the organization overall?

In another organization, a senior head of a major operating division was at odds with corporate headquarters and all the staff people who were at the corporate level. This very personal conflict placed all the people who reported to him in an extremely awkward position. Did they actively participate on various task forces that were assembled with representatives from each of the operating divisions? Did they cooperate with initiatives that came from corporate headquarters? Did they take any initiative to interact with their counterparts in other divisions? The answer was most often no, and that caused an enormous drain on the effectiveness of the overall corporation.

Such interpersonal conflicts seem reminiscent of teenagers in high school and their social dynamics. You could laugh at how childish these squabbles were if they didn't have such a destructive impact on organizational achievement and efficiency.

POSITIVE EFFECTS OF TEAM DYNAMICS

For most people, there is an excitement and energy that comes from being part of a team, even for those who seem highly independent and often are solo performers.

One of the most dramatic moments of the 2008 Olympics was when the U.S. men's swim team came from behind to win the 4×100-meter team medley final. The hero of the Olympic games, Michael Phelps, was on the deck of the pool with teammates Garrett Weber-Gale and Cullen Jones, cheering wildly as Jason Lezak chased down Alain Bernard of France in the last 15 meters to win the gold medal. Swimming, of course, is a highly individual sport, but there was more excitement in the team event than in any other at Beijing's Water Cube. Most of the swimmers had competed against each other during the meet, but the joy and excitement of having a teammate succeed was tangible. They appeared to be having far more fun sharing the team success than was ever evident when they were swimming alone in various meets. Phelps summed it up simply after the race when he said, "The team events are the funnest!"

CONCLUSIONS FROM RESEARCH

So what practices can you initiate that will foster this team spirit and collaboration in those who report to you?

Minimize Competition

One of the assumptions guiding some organizations is the belief that if you want to get the best people to work their hardest, the surest way is to set up two or more competing groups. Give them the same challenge. Yes, some feathers will be ruffled, and maybe even some fur will fly, but it will produce the best result in the shortest time. After all, life is all about winners and losers, and that's the price you pay for getting a great result. Do you agree?

Don't. Collaboration almost always wins over competition. As far back as 1954, Peter Blau of Columbia University studied two groups of interviewers in an employment agency. One group's members were highly competitive, were concerned primarily about their own productivity, and were highly ambitious. The second group was just the opposite. Its members were by nature collaborative and worked as a team. The second group's success in filling jobs was far better than that of the first.

Virtually every study that has been conducted on the impact of competition versus collaboration has shown that competition loses. Why? Success in today's world demands the sharing of information and resources. Competition erodes and finally destroys that. Competition breeds suspicion and hostility, which, in turn, actively discourage any sharing of information and resources. Furthermore, trying to do well for the overall organization and trying to beat an internal competitor are two totally different objectives. They cannot both be met at the same time.

Wise leaders are cautious about structuring competition between groups, realizing that unbridled competition often leads to conflict. Conflict, in turn, has enormously negative outcomes. Competition is an accepted, even revered, element of our society. People compete in sports. We compete in business. Our legal system brings competitive points of view together before a judge or jury. Most of the time the participants, whether they be athletes, corporate employees, or lawyers, can meet and be civil with one another and not have personal animosities arise.

But unbridled competition that persists over a long period of time leads to highly dysfunctional conflict. It often becomes personal. The game or the issue takes a backseat to emotion. Fights erupt on the field. Teams begin to engage in questionable practices (such as the videotaping of signals that the opponent's coaches are giving from the sidelines, as practiced by the New England Patriots) in order to obtain some advantage over others. Long-established rules of engagement are set aside in the heat of the battle. Even the fans supporting the teams, people sitting high in the stands and not butting heads on the playing field, become so emotionally wrought up that they pick fights, throw cups of beer on fans of the other team, and end up engaging in highly destructive behavior.

Social scientists have observed for decades that highly successful innovations that occur in one part of an organization are seldom adopted by others. One plant figures out a way to streamline the production of a device with 30 percent less cost. Other plants are manufacturing the same product. Reason would hold that the other plants would willingly embrace such successful innovations and readily implement them in their part of the corporation. While the reasons may be complex and many, the competition between divisions in corporations seems to be the single largest force keeping that from happening. People think to themselves, "I don't want a sister division to do well, especially if it makes us look bad." "We compete for resources against them."

> In the early days of Apple Computer, two competing teams were created to develop the next generation of computers. But a strategy that had been intended to accelerate the development of a new product ended up with the groups stealing resources from each other and building walls of silence in a wasteful and destructive manner. The Mac group won, but the internal cost was extremely high.

What's the lesson to be learned? Use competition sparingly. Keep the duration short. When it's over, bring the teams together to celebrate. Be certain that people inside the organization recognize your real competitor as the *real* competitor, and that it is never a sister division.

When leaders receive 360-degree feedback from their employees, we have observed that one of the most frequently occurring criticisms is about the leader's tolerance of conflict within the work group. People often express strong feelings about the need for the leader to step up and do something about the conflict that is tearing the group apart.

Make Teams the Basic Building Block of the Organization

What's the difference between a team and a randomly selected group of individuals? It starts with the members of a team having a common goal or purpose, and continues with their having some definition of roles and responsibilities. It often includes having some defined processes that govern how the team operates and communication channels that enable the team to function. Many forces combine to create effective teams, and the evidence is quite clear that team-based structures are becoming the standard. They generally perform better than a more traditional hierarchy.

Today's organizations, with their global reach and complex set of activities, are able to function because of two "structural materials."

The first is information technology, which makes it possible for companies to make timely information available to thousands of people simultaneously, no matter where they're located. The second technology is the innovative use of teams—not in the traditional sense, but as a basic building block of the new architecture, relying upon people to use their collective knowledge, judgment, skill, and creativity to perform a variety of jobs and functions, rather than just one, in concert with their colleagues.[1]

Teams aren't appropriate in every circumstance. But when the situation is right, teams have a broad range of beneficial results for the organization. Information flows more readily. Coordination between individuals is more seamless and easier. Decisions are made with greater rapidity, and all involved feel greater ownership in the outcomes because they have had a strong voice in the decisions. The ultimate execution and implementation of any project can be accelerated. The teams have structurally helped to create an organizational culture of collaboration.

The fear that many have about the concept of teams is that personal accountability will be diminished. They worry that the team will allow everyone to point a finger at several other people and say, "I'm not responsible; it's these other people." This is not how effective teams function. Rather than individual team members pointing at each other, the outcome has been that everyone on the team feels a great personal sense of responsibility for the output of the entire team. Instead of having one person feel responsible for making something happen, there is now a group feeling of responsibility for everything.[2]

Reward Team Effort and Accomplishment

The inspirational leader emphasizes the value and rewards for team effort. Many leaders push this concept aggressively, all the way to the creation of self-managing work teams, in which groups of seasoned employees take on many of the functions that would normally be performed by a supervisor or manager. Short of that, they do the following:

- Reward those who collaborate with others
- Coach those who hesitate in their collaboration with others
- Ask for team members to report in staff meetings on collaborative activities that are underway
- Praise colleagues for time spent assisting other divisions or departments
- Free people up to participate on corporate task forces or to support a sister division

In a large gathering of executives of a large sportswear corporation, senior executives asked some of the 450 people in attendance to stand up and report on activities in which one division had specifically helped another. Reports were greeted with cheers and applause. If you believe that what is rewarded gets repeated, then think of ways to spotlight acts of team effort and collaboration.

Assume that most front-line employees enjoy collaborating rather than competing.

Assume further that these employees have the good of the organization at heart, rather than merely that of their own department. Employees appreciate alignment between what they know is good for the organization and what their leader rewards. It is not surprising, therefore, that the leader who encourages team effort and cooperation will be far more inspirational than the leader who behaves the opposite way.

Dismantle Silos

The best leaders freely cross boundaries for the organization's good. Formal organization charts with lines and boxes describe reporting relationships and chains of accountability. They conveniently group functional activities, such as marketing, sales, and operations. But they completely fail to describe how organizations really function. One observer noted that while organizations appear to be groups of silos, the real work occurs in the horizontal pipes that connect them, either above or below ground. As the Total Quality Management movement took hold and helped organizations to greatly increase the quality of their products and services, one of its main conclusions was that approximately 85 percent of the inefficiency and waste in organizations did not happen within departments, but in the pass-off of activity from one group to another.

We were asked to coach an executive who had troubles in this arena. In our feedback session to him, we commented: "You are seen as pinning labels on people or groups, such as 'nonsupportive,' 'can't make up their minds,' or 'not pulling their weight.' What impact do you think this behavior is having on your direct reports and peers? Have you considered praising other groups in public. Focus on what they do well, and work to magnify that. If you have some criticism or complaint, go privately to them with that feedback."

Criticizing other groups in public has the effect of filling the horizontal pipes that connect the groups with quick-setting concrete.

We went on in coaching him: "Within the overall group reporting to you, it is perceived that there are subgroups that need to be brought together. That has been characterized as a 'veterans' group versus the rest of the organization. Would greater cohesion within the overall team produce some real benefit? People admire your standing up for what is best for your former employer, but they also think that issues between the groups are escalated more rapidly and with more amplitude than is needed."

This leader's behavior was not helping. Reinforcing the walls of the silos is never a good idea if the organization is depending on seamless interactions between groups.

Resolve Conflicts Quickly

When people live together, daily interactions can easily lead to misunderstandings and minor irritations. Some of the most interesting research in marriage counseling has shown that the biggest single predictor of those couples who ultimately end by divorcing is the absence of a problem-solving or conflict-resolving mechanism. Divorcing couples simply could not find ways to get over their differences amicably. Other couples experienced just as many or just as serious conflicts. Those who stayed married figured out ways to fix them.

That principle also applies inside organizations. Organizations get into trouble when conflicts fester and the leaders ignore this. We noted earlier that in our work providing multirater feedback to leaders in organizations, the two lowest scores received by most leaders are on "Practices self-development" and "Resolves conflicts within the work group."

It is unclear whether this comes from the following:

- Being unaware that the conflict exists
- Discomfort with stepping into such issues
- Inability to resolve conflicts

In addition to the normal discomfort with conflict, many of you who have been parents have attempted to resolve a fight between two children, only to have both children turn on you. Your efforts at adjudicating the battle ended up with you being the adversary of both of them.

Or, it could be that we don't know how to resolve the issue. With all that has been published by groups that have studied conflict resolution, the following concepts and appropriate behaviors seem straightforward and clear:

- Find common points of agreement.
- Agree on the principles underlying a good resolution of the dispute.
- Help people to move away from their "position" on an issue and focus on identifying their "interests." What is it that is important to them? Is there a way to help one group attain its interests, while simultaneously having the other group attain its interests as well?

- Create options that benefit both parties.
- Agree on the criteria that you will use to resolve the issue.

Involve the Right People in Decision Making

This leadership behavior appears to work in two ways. Looking at it from the perspective of any subordinate being studied, this behavior of involving the right people may mean that "my opinion is sought." If so, it is clear that having a leader seek my views on an important topic is highly motivating. It is an act that conveys respect and appreciation. It is a form of recognition. It strengthens the bond that I have with my leader. For a host of reasons, this is motivational.

Alternatively, if I am working on a project and seeking to move it along, my leader's willingness and help in getting the most knowledgeable and strongest people to help in the decision process is also highly motivating to me. Again, it moves the project forward at an even brisker pace. It signals that what I'm doing is important, and that it is for the overall good of the broader organization.

> History records innumerable examples of leaders being influenced by able teams and how this greatly enhanced their ultimate success. American history records several instances of General George Washington wanting to attack the British and being blocked by a strong cabinet. From every indication, viewing the events from a historian's perspective, the cabinet was absolutely correct. Attack would have been disastrous. More recently, the Cuban Missile Crisis that happened during John F. Kennedy's presidency showed the value of involving the right people.

However, successful teams require a highly disciplined process for decision making. The team needs to agree up front how it will go about making important decisions. This process defines how key decisions are identified, how information is collected, who will be involved, and the process by which a decision will be achieved.

Create an Inclusive Environment

One of the leadership acts that inspires and motivates is the willingness of leaders to help people feel that they are inside the organization as full-fledged members looking out to the rest of the world rather than being on the outside looking in. Leaders who are comfortable with diversity in race, gender, age, academic background, and general demeanor are far more inspirational to each individual who represents those differences than are leaders who are comfortable only with people who look and think like themselves.

In this way, the strengths of individuals are used. That in itself is highly motivating. Leaders clearly need to not play favorites and to put the well-being of the group above that of any one individual. However, the counterpart to that is the great gains that come from showing concern for each individual in the group.

> The power of an inclusive group to inspire and motivate people in the group is an ironic element for this book. We're analyzing what it is that leaders do that inspires. In this case, in an almost catch-22 process, the leader's creation of a cohesive team would seem to be circumventing our main objective. In reality, the cohesive team provides some of the strongest influence to perform at the highest level.
>
> The Marine on the battlefield would quickly acknowledge that he is primarily fighting for his comrades on either side of him, not for the captain or the general. It is the wise leader who recognizes this powerful force and who makes no attempt to get in the way of it.

COLLABORATION AND TEAMWORK ARE ULTIMATELY WAYS TO BUILD CULTURE

Collaboration and teamwork are norms that need to be established in the culture of the organization. For them to succeed, many other elements need to be in place.

Effective teams ideally require diversity of skills, talents, and experience, along with other kinds of diversity. The culture has to become one of putting the organization's and the team's interests higher than anyone's self-interest, no matter how senior that person is in the organization. Ideas and proposals have to be evaluated on their merits, not on the role power or position that their proponent holds in the organization. There is a far greater degree of empowerment for the people, and thus leadership is shared much more broadly through the organization.

STEPS TO TAKE

1. Strongly consider the advantages of creating a team-based structure rather than the traditional organization form of people working alone.
2. Minimize destructive conflict between groups. If you hear people taking potshots at another group, begin immediately to bring the groups together.
3. Don't pit groups against each other. Temporary contests can be fun and have a positive effect, but be cautious in dragging them out.
4. Reward team effort and accomplishment wherever possible. That encourages collaboration and cooperation.
5. Tear down silos. Remove the barriers that separate groups from one another.
6. For additional information and resources on collaboration and teamwork go to www.zengerfolkman.com and click on the Inspiring Leader icon.

Chapter 12

Fostering Innovation

The guy who invented the first wheel was an idiot. The guy who invented the other three, he was a genius.

—Sid Caesar

The way to get good ideas is to get lots of ideas and throw the bad ones away.

—Linus Pauling

I want to put a ding in the universe.

—Steve Jobs

Innovation is connected to inspiration. That is a statistical fact. Frankly, we were a bit surprised at the strong link between the two. We never would have predicted it. But in every organization that we studied, this factor jumped out. There is obviously something about a leader's encouraging innovation that has an extremely powerful impact on people. People are jazzed by the opportunity to participate in new and exciting activities.

What the leader did was create not only an environment in which people felt free to bring in fresh ideas, but, even better, an environment in which injecting new points of view was both strongly encouraged and expected.

Many of us have encountered the leader who finds a variety of reasons to resist any new ideas that come from someone else. They've been jokingly described as "abominable no-men." (We quickly acknowledge that some women deserve that description as well.) In some cases, it is because the leader likes things just as they are now. Much like the dread of buying a new pair of shoes that will be stiff and uncomfortable and require giving up the comfort of a well-broken-in older pair, the contemplation of new processes, new products, or new people can be disquieting.

In other cases, this attitude appears to be driven by pride or arrogance. The logic (or illogic) trail goes something like this:

> I'm the boss. Good ideas should come from me. I didn't think of it, so therefore it can't be a good idea. Worse yet, if I accept a subordinate's idea, someone in the organization might think my subordinate should be the boss. That is even more unacceptable, so obviously I cannot accept this idea.

Whatever the reason, leaders who resist ideas that don't come from themselves are all too prevalent in organizations.

WHAT THE INSPIRING LEADER SEEKS TO CREATE
A Dynamic Culture and Environment

Consider two working environments.

The first is extremely static. Things don't ever appear to change. The paint on the walls never changes. The office furniture never changes. The way paperwork is processed is identical to the way it was processed five years ago. People come in exactly on time, and they leave exactly on time. There are no sounds of laughter in the halls. Instead, the tone feels like a library of yesteryear. Everything is businesslike and buttoned-down. People appear to hibernate in their cubicles. The manager stays in her office, and staff members occasionally go in to discuss some matter they feel they can't decide alone.

The second environment is virtually the opposite. The new manager walks around the office and frequently asks about ways to do things better. Nothing seems off limits. He gives positive reinforcement for what is happening, and periodically asks, "Why do we need this form?" "What's the reason for this procedure?" "Have you considered any other ways of tracking customer usage of this product?" The tone of these questions is true curiosity, never accusatory. As project teams are created, office furniture is moved around, and people end up in new offices or cubicles in order to be nearer the people they work with. Several informal discussions take place, occasionally punctuated with loud laughter. Offices are decorated with personal objects and pictures obviously drawn by the employees' children. There is a tangible feeling of excitement that permeates people's activities.

In which environment would you be more inspired? (Yes, we agree. That's almost a silly question.) The climate in which change is encouraged, innovation is expected, and things are not regimented is far more inspiring to nearly all of us.

The takeaway for the reader is a recommendation to perform a realistic, frank analysis of the climate of the organization you manage. Does it more closely resemble the first or the second? Before considering any specific techniques or steps to take, reflect on the culture that's currently in place. If it has several elements of the first scenario, then take some steps to shake things up. Just as rearranging the furniture in your home or apartment serves to break the monotony, so little things make a big difference in an organization's culture. Ask trusted team members for suggestions as to what changes would make the most difference.

Innovation Happening at All Levels and within All Functions

General Electric has long enjoyed a reputation for forward thinking. Under Jack Welch, it was recognized for its decision to become number one or number two in each market it served, and if that was not possible, Welch wanted GE to get out. Its reputation was one of a strong focus on delivering results and operational excellence. Welch expanded the organization through diversification into new industries. He acquired countless new operations and divested companies that did not meet his standards for producing a positive return.

Upon Welch's retirement, Jeffrey Immelt was elected chairman and CEO of the firm. His emphasis shifted to a much stronger focus on innovation and internal growth. All executives were expected to come up with one or two bold initiatives that would grow their part of the business in a dramatic way. Small, incremental gains were to be augmented with serious innovation and growth plans that could have a significant impact on GE's bottom line. Immelt paid close personal attention to the top 20 projects that were selected by the management team to receive corporate support.

Innovation Becoming Embedded in the Systems

When the right environment is created and combined with the expectation that everyone will contribute to the innovation process, then a steady stream of good ideas for new products, services, marketing techniques, and ways to better manage the business come forth on a regular basis.

One of the most innovative organizations that many of us frequently encounter is a California company, OXO, that produces innovative kitchen utensils.

> Regina Schrambling wrote in the *Los Angeles Times,* "Ever since Oxo came out with a Good Grips vegetable peeler in 1990 that changed the way America prepped mashed potatoes, the company has become so known for its hyper-clever takes on everyday things that the wow factor should be increasingly difficult to come by."
>
> Visitors to the company's home office observe 40 employees dwelling on the details of various kitchen gadgets. The key to their success is that they really "sweat the small stuff." Every kitchen utensil is fair game for radical improvement. This all began when the founder, Sam Farber, modified some kitchen utensils for his wife, who suffered from arthritis. Now teams work for years trying to perfect a new product, and after it is released, they immediately begin analyzing what is wrong with it and how it could be improved. A new design is never good enough and is never off-limits for further improvement.

Over 500 products have been OXOized since those early days of the swivel peeler. It now comes in multiple styles, and one even has a replaceable blade.

"We never consider anything finished," said Larry Witt, OXO's vice president of sales and market development.[1]

Aim Is High and Not Satisfied with Tiny Steps

OXO is a good example of a focus on innovation that is not content with mere line extensions for old products or "me-too" products that copy a competitor. When the right climate is created, there are no restrictions on the boldness or scope of the proposed innovation. It could be a new market to pursue, a new product line to invest in, a better way to outflank a competitor, or a better way to go to market.

HOW LEADERS ACHIEVE THESE OBJECTIVES
Determine If You Personally Have a Yes or a No Approach to New Ideas

You may be surprised at what you discover. Leaders have a huge impact on the amount of innovation that occurs within their group. But this impact can be subtle. It is usually a summation of little things, no one of which blatantly stands out. Often leaders' behavior unwittingly closes down creativity and innovation.

There's a large number of leaders for whom the default answer to any suggestion is no. The first step we propose is that you collect some data from your subordinates about your impact on their attempts at innovation. After reading the written comments on 360-degree feedback instruments for thousands of leaders, it is striking to see the number who are seen as rejecting any idea that is not their own.

Discovering your receptiveness to new ideas requires asking your people some direct questions, either as a group or one on one. You can ask questions like these:

- "Do I ever say or do things that discourage people from proposing new ideas?"

- "Have you ever seen me react in a way that suggested that I wasn't eager to take a risk or try some new approach?"
- "To what degree do you think I want to get ideas from the group about new products or better ways we could work?"

While reflection and introspection may help, nothing compares to your asking people some probing questions and then patiently listening to the answers. This first step is important because many leaders who think they are open to new ideas are not seen that way by their subordinates. We virtually never see leaders describe themselves as rejecting ideas from their subordinates, but the subordinates see it quite differently.

> One leader who was somewhat aware of his behavior in this regard was a senior executive in a large multinational bank. He was responsible for all the organization's information systems and procedures. On a 360-degree feedback instrument, his subordinates gave him extremely low scores regarding his willingness to support innovation and his overall receptivity to new ideas. When we discussed this fact with him, his reply was: "My job is to keep this place from blowing up. Any change someone proposes has that potential. So my answer to any suggestion is always no. Then I'll ponder it some more, and if the person is really persistent, I may think about it and try it out in a very limited way."

You had to respect and admire this executive's feeling of responsibility for the welfare of the firm. But by his own assessment, his function, and therefore the entire bank, hadn't kept up with some of the innovations that competitors had embraced. This put the bank at some competitive disadvantage. There was a serious morale problem among those who reported to him. Turnover was unusually high. We talked about what would happen in a relatively short time when he retired.

We suggested, "What if you first pointed out all the good things about an idea that is proposed to you. Then, after letting the person know that you appreciate his initiative and his having thought about ways to improve things, you might ask him if he sees any potential downsides or dangers to his proposal. After he's given his answers, by all means add any important ones that you think he's missed. Then ask him whether, on balance, this still seems like a good idea. Maybe ask if he can refine his proposal to eliminate the risks and preserve its positive aspects. There are clearly ways to protect the company and, at the same time, to inspire and motivate your colleagues by encouraging innovation and risk taking." Shortly thereafter he retired. His legacy was one of having done good things, but it fell short of what it could have been had he been more receptive to the ideas that bubbled up from a talented staff.

This doesn't mean that ideas and suggestions should not be turned down. If they don't make sense, they should be rejected. But some managers automatically say no unless there is overwhelming evidence and pressure to say yes. We submit that this is the wrong default answer to people who have taken the time to think about a better way of doing things.

Remove the Barriers

Ask your subordinates what is standing in the way of their making suggestions and proposing new and better ways to get work done. You'll discover, in all likelihood, some things you hadn't imagined. Excessive paperwork and approvals may be one thing that's getting in the way. The lack of a clear channel by which to get new ideas considered may be another. Maybe the culture of the organization is resistant to new suggestions. Whatever you discover to be the barriers, take aim at them. Banish the bureaucracy that gets in the way.

Another skill that the inspiring leader possesses is one of internal marketing. Such a leader is skilled at helping others to see the problem or issue and how what is being proposed will solve that problem. The impact of a change is rarely confined to one department or group. Invariably the change spills over to other areas. Their agreement is required if this change is to succeed. This requires the leader's being perceived as working for the welfare of the entire organization, not just for something that will primarily benefit the leader's group.

Remove potential barriers. Because change usually affects many other groups, it is extremely important to identify the most likely barriers standing in the way of this change. Change efforts succeed when those responsible have taken the time to anticipate some of the key barriers and hurdles to making the change happen.

Open the Door

Overtly encourage innovation. Send a clear signal that you are receptive to innovative ideas. Frequently ask, "Is there a better way to get this done?" "How long has it been since anyone dissected this process to see if it can be streamlined?" In addition, borrow an idea from Jeffrey Immelt's playbook. Ask the people in your organization to come up with one or two really bold ideas that have the potential to transform the business. That means everyone.

Another reason that leaders sometimes resist innovation, we fear, goes back to the fundamental levels of respect that senior people have for those at lower levels. Some senior people assume that being promoted to a higher level equates to superior abilities, including a much higher IQ. Often, there is a generally higher level of education the higher in the organization you go. But in today's organization, our observation is that there are usually some extremely bright and well-educated people at lower levels. When senior people dismiss ideas from people at lower levels on the basis of some assumed superiority of the people at the top, this causes terrific ideas to be ignored. Worse yet, the leaders' not paying attention is very uninspiring to these people.

> Some leaders resist innovation and ideas because they believe that good ideas largely come from management. We earlier noted that this is simply not the case. But many leaders hang on to the mistaken belief that Jack Welch described as thinking that the law of gravity

applied to ideas. Some leaders believe that good ideas start at a high level and gently fall down to the layers below. One of Clayton Christensen's contributions from his research on innovation was that this idea was a complete fallacy. The best leaders stayed attuned to the ideas that bubbled up from below, identified those with the greatest merit, and then institutionalized them. This pattern can be identified in every successful organization and in most successful new products, whether it is Post-it notes or Intel's decision to manufacture microprocessors rather than transistors. (In hindsight, the decision to manufacture microprocessors and abandon the manufacture of transistors was an extremely good one. There are now more transistors produced each year than there are grains of rice, and the price per transistor is less than that of each grain of rice.)

In a large midwestern plant, the new management decided to transfer much more of the decision making and control to teams at the lowest level of the plant. After these changes were implemented, one of the workers went home to visit his father, who had worked in that same plant for nearly all of his working life. As the son described the innovative decisions that the employees were now making, including new systems for ordering materials and scheduling production runs, Internet programs for interacting with suppliers, and regular meetings to talk with customers, his father's eyes welled up with tears. He said, "I told 'em. We knew how to run that plant better than they did. We could have done all those things. If only we'd had the chance."

We wish those days were all in the past. But they are not. We regularly see senior management teams who, from our vantage point, seriously underestimate the capability of the group below them. That often comes from having minimal interaction with the people in that group. It also arises from not putting them in roles where they can be tested and prove that they can perform.

> On more than one occasion, we have worked with a senior team as its members participated in a rather challenging business simulation as part of their development process. The senior team had often been the pilot group for the organization, and it was followed in this development process by other teams that reported to it. These second groups usually perform well, sometimes better than their bosses. That was an important eye-opener and helped to create even greater confidence on the part of the senior team in their successors.

Create Forums in Which Innovative Ideas Can Be Discussed and Recognized

Set up forums in which innovative ideas can be explored, fully understood, and finally evaluated. Give positive reinforcement not only to the ideas that are accepted, but also to those that were tabled or turned down.

Some leaders mistakenly think that the only innovative ideas that deserve public acknowledgment and positive acclaim are those that are accepted and put into action. This is a mistake. Innovative ideas get put on the back burner for a variety of reasons that have nothing to do with the creator or the quality of the idea. It may be a matter of timing, funding, other projects that are extremely similar, or a variety of other reasons.

Our research shows clearly that inspiring leaders champion new projects and programs. The key here is that the leader who inspires is willing to take the initiative to get things started. Here are some examples of what this leader says or does:

- "How about figuring out a better process for customizing our products for our key clients?"
- "I want to change the format of our weekly meeting, and would like your ideas. I'm sensing that it could be a lot better than it is."

- "The software that we're using to manage our manufacturing process lacks some functionality that I'd like to have. How would you feel about searching for some better alternatives and coming back with some recommendations?"
- "We've been selling the same version of this product for years. We've heard many recommendations for ways to upgrade it, and we've all worried about the time and money it will cost, but we're not providing the best product that we know how to produce. The time has come, in my opinion, for us to bite the bullet and make the changes. Who agrees with that?"

> Organizations can be like the plate spinner's plate. As time passes, the plate revolves increasingly slowly. Then it begins to wobble. It needs a burst of energy to get it back spinning rapidly and horizontally. The leader's energy is often required to get things started.

Engage key stakeholders. One powerful technique the leader can use to make all this happen is to reach out to the key stakeholders who will be involved. The leader then floods other stakeholders with the information they'll need if they are to fully understand what is being proposed. The reasons for the proposed change are made clear. The effective leader helps key stakeholders see why this is in the best interests of the entire organization and the other surrounding groups that will be affected.

Set Up Processes That Support Innovation

Much has been published about the innovation process. Some of the most useful data come from design firms such as IDEO, which has published a great deal about the techniques it uses in the innovation process. These begin with a variety of ways to observe how customers use a product and the experience they are currently having. The techniques include in-depth interviews, shadowing customers, and photographing customers using the product. The second step is an intensive idea-generating meeting to brainstorm possibilities. The third step is a rapid prototyping phase in which mock-ups of either a product or a proposed service are made. These mock-ups are then tested in a variety of ways. After that comes a refining process in which the ideas are polished, new prototypes are created, and agreement is reached on a new design. Finally comes the implementation stage, in which a multidisciplinary approach is taken to plan and execute the implementation. IDEO's enormous success attests to the payoff from following this process rigorously.

Others are also pushing the boundaries of the innovation process. One of the more interesting comes from the work of a Russian scientist, Genrich Altshuller. His work is referred to as TRIZ, an acronym for the Russian phrase "theory of solving inventive problems" or "theory of inventive problem solving."

> Today, TRIZ is a methodology, tool set, knowledge base, and model-based technology for generating innovative ideas and solutions for problem solving. TRIZ provides tools and methods for use in problem formulation, system analysis, failure analysis, and patterns of system evolution (both "as-is" and "could be"). TRIZ, in contrast to techniques such as brainstorming (which is based on random idea generation), aims to create an algorithmic approach to the invention of new systems, and the refinement of old systems. . . .
>
> Altshuller was employed to inspect invention proposals, help document them, and help others to invent. By 1969 he [had] reviewed about 40,000 patent abstracts in order to find out in what way the innovation had taken place. He eventually developed 40 Principles of Invention, several Laws of Technical Systems Evolution, the concepts of technical and physical contradictions that creative inventions resolve, the concept of Ideality of a system and numerous other theoretical and practical approaches; together, this extensive work represents a unique contribution to the development of creativity and inventive problem-solving."[2]

One big lesson that emerges from the work of such groups is that innovation requires a process. Indeed, that process will nearly always look and feel very different from traditional processes embedded in organizations.

Shower Positive Attention on New Ideas

Never begin by enumerating all the downsides and potential problems. Be optimistic. New ideas are fragile. They are like tiny plants that poke its way up through the soil. Rough handling at this point can easily kill them, and lots of great ideas have been squashed at this stage.

For more than a decade, one of the authors worked in a pharmaceutical company. A senior executive in research, Ralph Dorfman, played a unique role in that organization. Whenever someone had a new idea for an innovative research project, she would go to Ralph. He was a respected scientist with a good deal of experience in research. But the spectrum of research being conducted ranged from molecular biology to chemistry and from biology to pharmaceutical science, with clinical medicine added on. Clearly Ralph was not the expert in all of these areas. But he possessed one quality that caused other people from virtually every area to come to spend time with him. He nurtured new ideas. He searched for the positive elements of everyone's brainstorm. By nature he was cheerful, always smiling and with a cherubic manner. His instinct was never to find fault and focus on the downsides, but to see the good and the potential in every new idea. One might assume that this was an observation that his colleagues would make years later as they reflected on the forces that made creativity possible. In Ralph's case, however, even at the time it was occurring, the scientists recognized what a valuable role he was playing in nurturing new ideas.

Make a Hobby of Trend Spotting

Encourage your group to stay out in front by spotting trends early. One of the behaviors of leaders who inspire is their ability and willingness to take an "eagle-eye view" of what's happening in their industry and to pick up on new trends at a very beginning stage. A good staff meeting topic is to ask about any trends employees are picking up as they talk with customers, industry experts, suppliers, and competitors and from what they are reading. The obvious next step is to determine what impact that trend could have on your business, or how you should best respond to it.

Visit Customers

Innovative products and services frequently originate from tips and suggestions from customers. Often customers will graciously toss these suggestions to you. But there is also great power in asking your customers some probing questions point-blank:

- "What would you like our product (service) to do that it doesn't do at the current time?"
- "Do you ever hear people in your organization talk about what they 'wish they had' in the realm of the work that we do?"
- "Would you mind if we spent some time talking to the direct users of our products (services) to hear from them firsthand the ideas for fine-tuning it that they might have?"

> Consider the rapid way in which an entire industry can be changed by a new idea. In 1989 Bob Plath, an airline pilot, was tired of carrying his luggage through the airport. He had the idea of combining a suitcase with a wheeled base. The first patent on a zippered suitcase with wheels and a telescoping handle was granted in June of 1990. Now more than 85 percent of travelers are using some version of a wheeled suitcase. Noticing that trend early could have spelled the difference between surviving and failing in the luggage industry.

Some industries are fortunate to have extremely long product life cycles. But that number is shrinking all the time. Product life cycles are shortening. The most effective leaders constantly scan their environment for subtle changes that may signal an important change. At the same time, they encourage all their colleagues to do the same.

One of the skills the inspirational leader needs to develop is to recognize when change is needed. Our research showed that those leaders who excelled at inspiration were far more adept at recognizing when the time had come for change to be implemented. It wasn't clear whether they were just more attuned to their environment or whether they were fundamentally more restless.

> Many of us have had the experience of living in a home or apartment for a few years. Then we have planned to have some company over or planned a party at our home. This made us look at our rooms with a more critical eye. There were spots on the carpet. The furniture was faded and frayed. The paint had some bad chips, and there was some water damage on the ceiling. Suddenly we saw our living space through a new lens. It triggered us to take some action. But it took some impending event to cause us to assess our living space objectively.

Create Events Focused on Innovation

There is great value in scheduling an off-site meeting for a team, away from the normal work environment, where the focus is exclusively on thinking about new products, new services, better methods of production, new ways to market, paths to better customer service, fresh approaches to pricing your products, and ways of improving the morale of the team. Having an outsider serve as facilitator of the meeting frees the leader to be an active participant, without the necessity of managing the group's process. That function can be temporarily delegated to the outside facilitator.

Have the Courage to Make Big Changes

Harvard Business School professor Clayton Christensen helped to catapult the issue of innovation to the forefront by publishing *The Innovator's Dilemma,* which was followed by a later volume, *The*

Innovator's Solution. Christensen achieved great notoriety through his analysis of how successful organizations must often launch products and services that will destroy their current offerings and how difficult and counterintuitive that is. His research showed that if they did not do it, others would, and then they would be in even greater difficulty. He contended that it was far better for a firm to take risks by launching products that might replace its current offerings than to stand by and have others cannibalize its market.

Making big changes requires courage. Recognizing that there is a need for change is obviously the first step, but change usually affects several people and often other departments. Unless there is external pressure on the leader to make some change, it is most often easier to let things continue as they are. But, as someone observed, "to follow the course of least resistance makes men and rivers crooked." The willpower to initiate change often begins with the leader.

We don't agree with the old saying that people resist change. It depends. Many people deliberately seek new experiences in specific parts of their life. They travel to new places. They take up new hobbies. They read new books. Comfort with change probably has a lot to do with how much control people feel they have.

Most of us resist having things done "to" us, especially if we lack control and if the outcomes are ambiguous or potentially damaging. So, if I hear that there will be a major reorganization in my work group, and if I have no knowledge of what is contemplated, it's probable that I'll be very resistant to the idea of that change. For additional resources to help inspiring leaders become more innovative and support innovation, go to our Web site www.zengerfolkman.com and click on the Inspiring Leader icon.

WHY FOSTERING INNOVATION AND RISK TAKING INSPIRES OTHERS

One of the most distinguished psychologists living has founded a movement known as Positive Psychology. It was meant to rebut the enormous preoccupation that psychology had with the darker sides of human nature. Martin Seligman's work[3] has had a profound impact on psychology. He resurrected the concept of character as a driving force in understanding individuals. With the help of equally distinguished colleagues, he researched the basic virtues and human strengths that permeate our culture. The six virtues they identified were ones that they found to be incorporated in all the major religious and philosophical traditions. Then, in order to have more workable and operational definitions of human character, they proceeded to identify 24 strengths that again seemed to cut across all cultures and societies.

Three of these strengths help to explain why innovation and risk taking would be inspiring to their recipients.

1. Curiosity/interest in the world. They defined this as "openness to new experience and flexibility about matters that do not fit one's preconceptions." "Curious people do not simply tolerate ambiguity; they like it."
2. Hope/optimism/future mindedness. This strength represents a positive attitude toward the future, expecting that good things will happen to you, provided you work hard, and emphasizing the importance of planning for the future.
3. Ingenuity/originality/practical intelligence/street smarts. The researchers defined this as a desire to find novel behavior to reach a goal. People who excel at this are not content with acting in a conventional way.

Our conclusion is that the desire to innovate and take risks is deeply embedded into our fundamental character. When it is denied, we feel great frustration and loss. When it is enabled, we feel greatly fulfilled and energized. The leader who does not allow and encourage innovation and risk taking obviously throws a wet blanket over the work group, whereas the leader who does the opposite unleashes the bottled-up energy and enthusiasm that exists within all of us.

Seligman writes:

> I believe that each person possesses several signature
> strengths. These are the strengths of character that a
> person self-consciously owns, celebrates, and (if he or
> she can arrange life successfully) exercises every day in
> work, love, play, and parenting. . . .
>
> Herein is my formulation of the good life: Using
> your signature strengths every day in the main realms of
> your life to bring abundant gratification and authentic
> happiness.[4]

STEPS TO TAKE

1. Take an objective look at your work environment. Is it
   dynamic, or has everything been fixed in place for a long time?
   What could you do to "loosen it up"?
2. Communicate the expectation that you have for innovation to
   occur at all levels and throughout your sphere of influence.
3. Design systems that encourage innovation. Discover elements
   of the culture or approval processes that have the having the
   effect of choking off new ideas.
4. Expect your senior leaders to propose bold initiatives that
   would have the potential to transform your business. Create
   that as an annual target.
5. Discover whether you have a yes or a no approach to new
   ideas. Use some of the questions proposed earlier in this
   chapter.
6. Identify the barriers that get in the way of innovation, whether
   they are approval processes or forms to complete.
7. In staff meetings and one-on-one conversations, open the
   door to suggestions for better ways to do everything.
8. Publicly recognize those who propose new ideas, regardless of
   whether these ideas were implemented or not.

9. Design a process that will encourage and support innovation in the organization. Adopt the techniques of organizations like IDEO that help innovation to happen.
10. Take time to discuss trends that you and your colleagues are seeing and discuss the best ways to respond.
11. Visit customers frequently. Ask them probing questions about what they'd change in your products or services.

Chapter 13

Most Common Mistakes in Inspiring Others

In George Lucas's epic sci-fi film *Star Wars: The Empire Strikes Back,* the character Yoda is a teacher of a universal energy called the Force. As Yoda instructs the saga's protagonist, Luke Skywalker, about how to use the Force, he admonishes him during a moment of despair, "You must unlearn what you have learned."

In few places is this more applicable than in helping leaders understand some bad habits in dealing with their subordinates and colleagues that they've acquired and that typically do not work when it comes to motivation. Leaders are often unconscious of the impact of many of their negative behaviors. The first real challenge is to become aware of these issues, and the second is to unlearn the behaviors that have evolved into detrimental habits.

In this chapter, we explore many of these critical errors that leaders make. Our hope is that any reader who might benefit from catching a glimpse of behaviors that he's only dimly aware of will find this useful. It should be obvious that leaders need to unlearn these behaviors. In one way, we're proposing an intensive "detoxification" for toxic bosses' bad behavior. We hope that you're guilty of none of these, but if you are the typical reader, chances are that some tiny bit of this applies to you.

WE SOMETIMES FAIL TO RECOGNIZE WHAT KILLS INSPIRATION AND MOTIVATION

One of the more common approaches to motivating people to higher performance is the leader who puts intense pressure on her people to perform. That pressure most often comes in the form of instilling a fear of the consequences of not performing. The first evidence that we could find of the use of this as a motivational tactic came from the Roman legions and the practice of decimation.

This practice was a form of military discipline used by officers in the Roman army to punish mutinous or cowardly soldiers. The word *decimation* is derived from a Latin term meaning "removal of a tenth," and the practice was used to punish the legion as a group. In some cases individual soldiers were punished, but decimation was punishment for the group. It was assumed that it would inspire fear and build greater resolve within the remaining troops.

If a legion had not performed up to the standard that was acceptable to the general, it was selected for decimation. The legion was divided into groups of 10. Within each group, lots were drawn, and the soldier who "drew the short straw" was put to death by the other nine. The theory was that obviously no legion would like this to happen to it, so the legions would perform at a very high level in order to avoid it.

In practice, however, decimation led to complete disintegration of the esprit de corps of the unit. It was a hard thing to watch comrades be killed by an enemy. But being forced to both watch and participate in the slaughter of comrades, not by the enemy, but by their own hand, caused the soldiers to completely lose their resolve to fight as well as their trust in their commanders.

While not nearly as gruesome, the modern-day version of decimation has been popular in some companies, including GE under Jack Welch's leadership. GE's strategy was to eliminate the bottom 10 percent of the workforce each year. While we are not interested in picking a fight with Jack Welch, we contend that this method of improving corporate performance is not as effective as focusing on what could be done with the middle 80 percent of the organization by helping them to perform like the top 10 percent. We would agree that if coaching, performance management, and other development efforts can't rectify the performance deficiencies of that bottom 10 percent as measured against some absolute standard, then it is better for those people to move on. But arbitrarily taking out the bottom tenth of every organizational unit, without regard to the unit's overall effectiveness in achieving its goals, seems to be both unwise and unfair. When measured against an absolute standard of effectiveness, it is possible that ultimately 20 percent of one group should be removed, while in many other groups, it could be that no one should be terminated.[1]

> We see many leaders who continue to behave in ways that backfire altogether. In the 2008 Olympics, U.S. pole vaulter Jenn Stuczynski, competing in the pole vault in her first Olympics, came in second after Russia's Yelena Isinbayeva, who took the gold medal while setting an Olympic record. You would think that Stuczynski's coach would be thrilled that she had been second only to Isinbayeva, who had won 14 consecutive major competitions.
>
> But after her final pole vault, the camera's picked up coach Rick Suhr mercilessly criticizing Stuczynski, pointing out all of the errors she had made in winning the silver medal and shrugging his shoulders with disdain. In what could have been a moment of triumph, Rick Suhr turned a moment of excitement into one of humiliation and brought Jenn Stuczynski to the brink of tears on national television. He ended his tirade not with congratulations, but by checking his BlackBerry e-mail.
>
> Even NBC's commentators were taken aback by his negative tone, asking, "Didn't she just win the silver medal? Where's the joy?"

Recognizing that there are a lot of different ways in which leaders are uninspiring, the following discussion identifies those behaviors that do the most damage when it comes to thwarting our efforts to inspire and motivate others.

THE UNINSPIRING LEADER

Our data were very compelling on the impact of the effectiveness of leaders when their development focus was on building strengths.

But that also caused us to ask the question, "Can people just ignore their weaknesses?" We found that there was a big difference between something we might call a weakness (a skill that a person is not very good at) and a *fatal flaw* (a profound weakness that overshadows everything that a leader does well and that can have a negative career impact). Even the best leaders have a few weaknesses or rough edges. We found that in most cases, leaders could ignore these and focus on building their strengths. When leaders have a fatal flaw, however, they need to correct it quickly because it is limiting their effectiveness and jeopardizing their career.

Behaviors of this kind become clearer when there are sharp contrasts. With that in mind, we analyzed more than 7,000 leaders and identified those who were in the depressing category of "least inspirational." These were the leaders in the lowest 10 percent of all the leaders being studied on the dimension of being inspirational. The question was simply, "What were they doing that caused them to be so uninspiring?" We wanted to understand what gets in the way of inspiration and to find a path forward for "unlearning" these behaviors.

Additionally, this analysis confirmed the essence of our research on the positive side of the inspirational equation. As you read this chapter about the uninspiring things that leaders do, you will no doubt see that some of them are simply behaviors that are the opposite of those that inspire. This fortifies our conclusions about the strengths we highlighted for the most inspiring leaders. It also provides a "view from below" of the issues that ultimately become barriers to our ability to inspire.

Note that uninspiring behavior is certainly just as powerful in pushing people in the negative direction—probably even more so. We all understand intuitively that it takes a great number of positive interactions to erase a negative interaction.

THE TOP 10 UNINSPIRATIONAL BEHAVIORS

So what does it take to have a nearly complete "charisma and inspiration bypass"? When we analyzed the data, the following emerged as the most detrimental behaviors. These 10 behaviors represent the most common failure points of leaders who lack that inspirational edge. In our research to uncover what the uninspiring leaders were doing differently, we found that it was a combination of the absence of desirable inspirational behaviors and the presence of some behaviors that were downright uninspirational. Like so many of the positive influencing attributes of inspiration, many of these behaviors work together in reverse to provide combinations that completely strip out motivation and inspiration from the workplace.

They Lack Energy or Enthusiasm

When these people walk into the room, you feel the energy leave. They absorb and consume energy, rather than injecting it into the group. To them, work simply feels like work rather than like a goal, a cause, or an opportunity to do something meaningful.

> One senior manager we worked with while doing some executive coaching received feedback that he literally "sucked the life out of meetings" with his lack of energy and enthusiasm about what the team was working on. The manager was competent in all of the technical areas of his job and was otherwise a reasonably affable person. But having very low energy and lacking a demonstrable passion about accomplishing a mission when you are the leader is a recipe for demotivation.

Don't misunderstand; this is not about being a cheerleader. Nobody said that leaders have to do cartwheels to get people's attention and motivate them. But let's face it, how much more enjoyable is it for people to work with leaders who are positive and energetic about what they are doing than to work with ones who are not? Which type of person do you want to work for each day, and which type makes you feel energized about the job that needs to be done?

Poor leaders fail to enthuse and excite their people. Our data provided a clear message that lacking energy and enthusiasm is a detriment that leaders can ill afford.

They Rarely Provide Clarity of
Direction or Purpose

With these leaders, team members are not clear about their goals or how they contribute to the success of the organization. The leaders provide no vision for where the organization is headed or what value the organization creates for others. They tell people what to do, when to do it, and how to do it, and they believe that this is all that is necessary for people to be productive and satisfied with their jobs.

Many leaders struggle with this, though not necessarily in the way you think they might. Leaders routinely spend significant amounts of time and resources defining and refining vision statements (or mission statements, divisional vision statements, or other such documents), but then do little or nothing to make all these grandiose words operational. Don't get us wrong; we are big believers in having well-crafted vision and mission statements. Where leaders fail is in their ability to break that vision down to the individual components for every person in the company and clarify how each person's work brings that mission statement to life. They fail to be clear about how the achievement of individual goals and milestones contributes to the greater achievement of these broad company objectives.

The inability of leaders to do this well prevents them from being able to cascade the power of these missions and visions throughout an organization or division. This lack of attention to clarifying direction and purpose for members of a team ultimately leads to cynicism about these visions and missions. The people who work for these leaders end up feeling little or no connection to or purpose for the ultimate contribution of their work. That leaves them feeling anything but inspired to go the extra mile.

They Avoid Setting Challenging Goals or Objectives

The lowest 10 percent of leaders do what needs to be done, but they always work hard to lower the expectations of others. They sandbag estimates of the time needed to complete projects to ensure that they will get projects done on time.

> Bill was the development manager working with computer programmers in a medical services company. He was getting very tired of being raked over the coals every month because his team had failed to deliver on its requirements. His solution was to use his basic math skills and do some multiplication. When new requirements came in, he and his team would estimate the time required to do the work, and then he would multiply the result by 2; if he felt that the request was more complex, he would multiply it by 3. To ensure that everyone was aware of how hard the team was working, he made a very long list of all the different projects that the team was working on. When people said that they needed a project done more quickly, he would pull out the list and ask, "What do you want to take off the list?" Bill's new approach worked extremely well. His people were more satisfied, and they had a more balanced work life. Everything seemed to be great until a competitor came out with a new release of a competitive product. It had many of the same features that Bill's team was developing, but his best estimate for completing the product was one year away. After a brief review of the product and the strength of the competition, the company decided to drop out of this market and concentrate its attention in other areas. Bill and his team were all laid off.

Most business leaders have heard the term BHAG (Big Hairy Audacious Goal), popularized in Jim Collins's book *Built to Last*. The reason that BHAGs are so effective at galvanizing support and commitment to a goal is that they help people to connect their work to an outcome that is of genuine significance. In our work over the years, it has become clear that the majority of people in the workforce are looking for greater purpose in their work. Collins's synthesis of why BHAGs are effective confirms that experience and essentially says that one of the ways in which great leaders inspire others to overachieve is by providing them with a clear sense of purpose and significance in the achievement of a goal.

Those leaders who are simply treading water or setting goals that are not truly challenging to achieve miss out on a powerful tool for inspiring those whom they lead. In fact, people work harder, perform better, and have more fun when they are working toward an objective, goal, or purpose rather than just getting through the month, quarter, or year.

They Have No Plan for Personal Development

These leaders assume that their skills are sufficient just as they are. They need no development, because if they weren't nearly perfect, then they wouldn't be in their current position.

In some cases, these leaders think they have all the skills they need to do their job effectively. In other, less arrogant cases, they may simply be too overwhelmed or task-focused to even think about where they might be able to improve. Where one might say, "I don't have time to do anything for my own development," the other does not even consider that he may need to prioritize his own development. In either case, not giving attention to a personal development plan affects the leader's ability to inspire.

> Sue was an executive vice president for an oil company. She had risen in the ranks over the years to her current position, where she reported to the president of the company. Sue was incredibly smart and a very hard-driving leader, but she had a tendency to either micromanage people or ignore them, which inevitably stalled decisions because nothing could be done without her approval. The president liked the way Sue paid so much attention to everything that was happening in the business, but her direct reports were constantly frustrated with her management style and approach.
>
> After hearing the president's praise of Sue, her direct reports had concluded that he was completely unaware of how she was stifling the business. Then the president decided that leaders in the company would go through

some leadership development, including a 360-degree assessment of their skills. When Sue's direct reports heard about this development process, it gave them some hope that Sue might finally get the message. The vice president of human resources was put in charge of designing a roll-out plan for the leadership development and started by meeting with each of the senior vice presidents. The human resources vice president was well aware of Sue's reputation and approached the interview with some trepidation. She was very surprised at Sue's interest in and support for the process. Sue indicated that she wanted all her managers to go through the program as soon as possible because "they needed the development." The human resources vice president then asked Sue, "Do you want to attend the program with the rest of your staff?" Sue indicated that this seemed to be a development process designed for lower-level managers and didn't really fit the needs of a person at her level. To clarify, the human resources vice president asked more directly, "So you won't be attending?" Sue replied, "I am far too busy!"

Interestingly, our studies showed that those leaders who are strong in self-development are very frequently rated highly on their ability to coach and develop others. The obvious conclusion here is that if you take care of your own development, you are perceived as being focused on how your people are growing as well.

They Provide No Coaching or Mentoring

The least inspiring leaders lack interest in helping other people develop new skills or capabilities. People are to do their jobs and be happy to get a paycheck. These leaders feel no obligation to develop people for future assignments. Often they feel stuck in their own jobs and justify not developing others because their leader has given them no idea about their future.

One of the most highly correlated drivers of employee commitment was the degree to which employees felt that they were developed and coached. As a result, it is no coincidence that the absence
of this driver ends up on this list.

Jack Welch describes this in his book *Winning* when he writes
about how important it is for a leader to "think of yourself as a gar-
dener, a water can in one hand and fertilizer in the other." Leaders
who view every moment as a teaching moment provide great
coaching and mentoring to those whom they lead. Failing to do
this or paying too little attention to this important function of a
leader is a crucial mistake.

> A high-technology company was several months into a
> major software upgrade on one of its network servers.
> Work had not progressed well, and James, the senior
> manager in charge of the project, was very frustrated. He
> had several meetings a day with various development
> teams, but he always came back shaking his head. Finally,
> a long holiday weekend arrived. The programming staff
> was elated. They had been working 60-hour workweeks,
> and James overheard all the chatter about a variety of
> plans from his entire staff about a mini-vacation. As James
> went home that night, he had never been so frustrated.
> His team members just didn't get it, and the work that
> they were delivering did not impress him.
>
> The long weekend passed, and as everyone returned to
> work, they noticed that the office where James worked
> was dark. He was always the first one to arrive and the last
> to leave the office. Team members joked that perhaps the
> long weekend break was not enough of a mini-vacation.
> The office was vacant all day. Since James was single, by
> afternoon his admin became concerned and called his
> home, but no one answered. The next day the office
> remained dark and empty. By the end of the week, HR
> had contacted local hospitals because no one had heard

from James. It was not until the end of the next week that James returned to work. As soon as his staff arrived, he called a meeting. James expressed appreciation for the concern about his absence. When asked, "Where have you been?" James replied, "I locked myself in the basement with my computer. I was working 20 hours a day and sleeping on a cot by my computer, but I've finished the application and it works beautifully. I knew I could do it. Now, let me show you what a real upgrade looks like."

It is impossible to know James's motivation for stepping in, but his motivation is not the issue. His people were clearly demotivated by his "yo-yo" approach of yanking back a key task from them. Worse yet, the team did not improve its ability to deliver. And when the next project is underway, the team's effort will most likely be half-hearted, knowing that James may take over without warning.

One of our clients who is the executive vice president of human resources at one of the largest companies in the world sums this up well when he states, "Our organization has leaders who are great users of talent but poor developers of talent." How inspiring is it to work for a leader whose priority is using your talent rather than developing your talent?

They Gunnysack Critical Information

These leaders prefer to control information and share as little as possible.

Sometimes these leaders are intentionally hoarding information, believing it to be a means of gaining and maintaining power. This sounds Machiavellian, but it happens. This is the stuff that brings negative connotations to office politics.

James was the CEO of a small start-up company. He was always very careful about what information he would share with the company. When he was encouraged to share the company financial data, his point of view was, "If everyone knew how much money we were making, then they would not work harder and would want raises. And besides, it is none of their business."

Sometimes those leaders are just not aware that other people would truly benefit by being included. They read and discard a memo, thinking that it applies only to them, or they are simply too absorbed in tasks and don't want to take the additional time needed to be inclusive. Sharing information with the team helps people feel connected to the company and clear about what is happening in the organization. It supports them in terms of both the quality of the work they are doing and how they feel about being part of the team.

They Say One Thing and Do Another

These leaders are hypocrites and don't walk their talk. This is, of course, in contrast to our earlier discussion about the importance of being a good role model.

> A few years ago, one of the authors worked with a senior executive in a small consulting firm. The company was going through significant cutbacks in spending, and one of the areas being addressed was travel costs. The president of the firm was definitive in his communication of the new expense policies. However, there was one senior executive who gave verbal support to the importance of keeping travel costs down, yet who stayed in Four Seasons or Ritz-Carlton hotels when he traveled, while other staff members stayed in more reasonable business hotels. Most people in the company resented his behavior, and while the financial impact of his behavior was probably not significant, consider the impact of this uninspiring behavior on those who tried to be fiscally responsible with their travel arrangements and the message that this leader was sending to everyone in the organization.
>
> When the new expense policies failed to produce any significant savings, the president lamented that nobody

understood how serious he was about this issue. He was incorrect; everyone understood how serious he was about this financial issue—it was just that a very visible senior manager behaved completely differently, and therefore others deemed any change in their own behavior unnecessary.

They Encourage Conflict and Competition with Other Groups or Individuals in the Organization

While this is a common affliction among leaders in large organizations, it happens in small companies too when leaders reinforce the silos between different groups. It is seen most often when leaders are focused on their own "turf" instead of on achieving company or business unit objectives. It frequently happens when they are fearful that the success of others will limit their success or the success of their team. When they behave this way, there is a complete absence of collaborative behaviors as they fight over resources or fail to cooperate with cross-functional processes.

For the people who work for the leaders of these work groups, the experience is miserable. The written comments in our database of several hundred thousand assessments from these team members say things like, "My job is more difficult because my boss makes everyone else angry." Or "Nobody seems to work together to achieve our goals—it's everyone for himself." How inspired do those folks sound?

They Have Little or No Interest in Ideas or Input from Their Direct Reports

Unsuccessful leaders discourage the involvement of the group. Their ideas take precedence. They believe that all ideas follow the law of gravity, starting from the highest point and gradually falling down through the organization to the lowest level. The idea of a senior executive going to a front-line worker and asking for ideas about improvements in the organization would be ludicrous.

Christine was in charge of a group of professionals. She approached her job in a very formal and disciplined way. She assigned work, provided direction on how it should be done, and regularly followed up on progress. Christine made it clear with all her direct reports that she expected the work to be completed according to her specifications. She never asked for input or suggestions from team members. After starting a new project, Jim, one of Christine's direct reports, thought he might have a good idea that would help the project move faster. He scheduled a meeting with Christine, but she indicated that her schedule was too tight to arrange an unplanned meeting.

Without thinking much about it, Jim scheduled a meeting with Christine's manager. He was happy to meet with Jim and listened openly to Jim's suggestions. He thanked Jim for taking the initiative. The next morning, when Jim arrived at work, he noticed that the message light on his phone was blinking. The message was from Christine, and it asked Jim to come to her office immediately. When Jim arrived, Christine quickly shut the door, looked Jim in the eyes, and said, "Never do that to me again." Jim was confused: "Do what?" Christine then said, "Go over my head and talk to my manager. He does not understand what we are doing here. Your idea will never work!"

Jim listened very well. He never made another suggestion, and he also taught all of his team members the painful lesson that he had learned.

They Rarely Provide Helpful Feedback on Performance

These leaders give people ratings but no reasons. They withhold feedback until the mandatory annual formal review, and then use it primarily as a rationale for lowering compensation or bonuses.

An example of this comes from the annual Bad Boss competition
by Working America, an affiliate of the AFL-CIO. Here's the story
from a woman named Joan in Kansas:

> Several years ago when I was the office manager at this
> company my boss asked me to organize an outing for
> our employees and I agreed. I felt an evening at a major
> league baseball game would be ideal for everyone.
>
> I set the date for about two months out, getting a
> reduction on tickets for a group, getting a set amount of
> cash to give each employee so they could purchase
> snacks, organized carpooling, handing out tickets, etc.
>
> The date arrived and it rained! My boss informed me
> that I had picked that particular date because I knew it
> would rain! My title changed from Manager to Assistant
> Manager and I was given a small reduction in pay.
>
> A few months later, he asked if I would like to
> organize a picnic. I told him no. He then informed the
> Board that I refused to organize an employee picnic!

CONCLUSION

As you review this list, we encourage you to take a moment for some
self-reflection. Perhaps you see yourself, even just a little, in some of
these illustrations. If you find that any of these items describes your
behavior, then this is the starting place for you to become more inspirational. These common failures of leaders to inspire come in several
forms; sometimes it is the absence of one of the positive inspirational
qualities, while other times it is an overt behavior that rests on mis-
guided assumptions or even being unaware of the impact of one's
behavior. Sometimes they are simply hypocritical or bad behaviors. As
human beings, we are all guilty of making such errors from time to
time, but they need not become fatal flaws if we are attentive to them.

Leaders with such weaknesses need to improve. The good news
is that positive improvement on any of these items, and the other
items that we've addressed in detail throughout the book, will have
a significant impact on your ability to lead others.

Chapter 14

Conclusions

I would not give a fig for the simplicity this side of complexity, but I would give my life for the simplicity on the other side of complexity.

—Oliver Wendell Holmes

What has made the study of inspiration so formidable has in part been that it is complex. But there was more that got in the way. The concept of motivation was cloaked in mystery. Words like *charisma* that were used to describe it were a rather public acknowledgment that "we don't understand this, and it is beyond the realm of analysis." That combination of complexity and inscrutability placed this topic completely out of bounds until just recently.

One of the truisms about the art of magic is that when you've learned the secret to how the magician made the object vanish, the selected card appears in the sealed envelope, or the coin magically move from one hand into the spectator's pocket, it's most often very simple. You mentally chide yourself for not having either observed or thought of the simple method that the magician used. But until you've learned the secret, it continues to be extremely deceiving.

We find that this same phenomenon applies to our study of inspiration. When you deal with it as an unsolvable mystery, you can enjoy watching someone do it, but it doesn't do much to help you. You make no progress in becoming inspirational, any more than the spectator who watches the magician cut the lady in half is making any progress in learning how to cut a lady in half.

But if the spectator knows the secret and has the equipment with which to practice, then watching someone else do it can be extremely valuable.

When you conclude that inspiration is not really a mystery, but something that can be understood and learned, then the topic takes on an entirely new dimension. So what's the bottom line? For the sake of simplicity, we'll attempt to boil down our conclusions to a relatively small number of ideas. We hope these are the primary messages that you have extracted from this book as you have read through it.

CONCLUSIONS

Stripped to their bare bones, the conclusions are as follows:

1. *Inspiration is a powerful component of the leader's repertoire.* It is the most powerful of all the differentiating competencies based on several different ways of determining importance. That is,
   - It is the competency that is most predictive of which leaders are given the highest overall ratings by their direct reports, peers, and boss.
   - It is the quality that employees most value in their leader. It is what they wish their leader to be.
   - It correlates most highly with employee commitment and satisfaction scores.
2. *It works as a catalyst.* It is not sufficient in and of itself. Its power comes when it is placed in combination with other leadership attributes. When inspiration is combined with behaviors like "drives for results" or "strategic thinking," then nearly miraculous things begin to happen.
3. *Inspiration is seldom "one thing."* It is the combination of many behaviors on the leader's part. You can picture these elements as rungs on a ladder, but without regard to order. The more rungs there are, the taller the ladder. Each in turn enables the leader to climb to higher and higher levels of influence.

These rungs include:
- Setting stretch goals
- Creating vision
- Setting clear direction
- Communication
- Teamwork
- Innovation

Because these are rather specific behaviors, they lend themselves to being learned as skills. No single one of them is mystical or impossible to attain. Indeed, some leadership development programs have been addressing these components of inspiration separately for some time, with reasonable success.

4. *While each rung is able to stand alone, it appears that the combination of several of these rungs is responsible for the more dramatic improvements produced by the highly inspirational leader.* You can arrange the rungs in varying combinations and permutations and get extremely positive results. The real power of these elements is in the effect of their combined interaction.

5. *Leaders vary in the inspirational techniques they prefer to use, and different techniques appeal to different colleagues.* Some approaches are obviously more comfortable than others for any given leader. Beyond that, the actions that inspire one person may not inspire another. Different people respond to different methods of inspiration.

6. *Inspiration works best when it has an end goal or purpose.* It brings positive changes into the behavior and attitudes of the entire organization. Specifically, it lifts productivity, increases self-confidence, enhances optimism and hope, expands the amount of initiative, and encourages higher levels of responsibility on the part of everyone. It also generates higher levels of enthusiasm and enables people to be more resilient and bounce back from any adversity.

7. *Inspiration is highly contagious.* Humans are highly influenced, both negatively and positively, by the emotions of other people who are proximate to them.

8. *Because of the formal positions of leaders, their emotions have a dramatically compounded degree of influence upon their subordinates.* The "role power" of leaders multiplies the effect of both their behavior and their emotions, almost as if others were experiencing them through a magnifying glass.

9. *Highly inspirational leaders have some attributes that reflect their acceptance of their leadership role and what it entails.* Specifically, they realize that all eyes are upon them. Like it or not, they are role models. Along with that, they must be the ones who champion change and keep the organization fluid by continually taking the initiative. Leaders who are not willing to accept the roles that leadership imposes upon them are not highly inspirational.

10. *The central core of inspiration is human emotion.* Inspiration primarily affects how people feel inside. Getting there may entail giving them new ideas or triggering new actions, but the end result has to be some stirring within the individual. It uncorks energy and passion that had been bottled up.

STEPS YOU CAN TAKE

Finally, here is our list of some actions that every leader should consider as ways to inspire and motivate the troops. We've chosen some of our favorites from earlier chapters in the book.

1. *Use emotions more frequently.*
   - Express heartfelt appreciation.
   - Get excited about a success in the organization.
2. *Reach out to people.* Initiate conversations and interactions.
3. *Set an aggressive target.* With the involvement of your team members, set a target that will stretch the group.

4. *Create a vivid picture of the organization three years from now.* Get each person to identify how this affects her job.
5. *Practice lavish communication.* Set up mechanisms by which you get feedback on how people are reacting to your communication.
6. *Delegate tasks with the development of the other person in mind.*
7. *Create positive consequences for having a personal development plan in place and for pursuing it.*
8. *Schedule regular coaching sessions with each subordinate.*
9. *Involve more people in decision making* on every important issue.
10. *Immediately identify and resolve conflicts within your team.*
11. *Set the expectation for innovation from everyone.*
12. *Shower positive attention on new ideas.*
13. *Schedule sessions with customers expressly for listening to their ideas.*
14. *Be the example.* Demonstrate to your colleagues with your actions what is valued by the organization.
15. *Take the first step.* Be the one to initiate changes, projects, or communication that is necessary for the organization.

Implementing even one of these suggestions will elevate your influence and inspire your subordinates to produce at higher levels. Implementing several of them will have a compounding effect on your ability to inspire and motivate others.

At the start of this book, we noted that considering all a leader has to do is a daunting task when you look at a job description that includes meeting financial objectives, achieving organizational or divisional goals, implementing changes, and managing a team, and then realize that while doing all of this, the leader also has to be inspirational.

Our sincere hope is that as you have read this book, we were able to decode for you just what it means to inspire and motivate others, and also provide you with practical and tactical methods for doing so. Now it is up to you to put it all into practice. The research is unequivocal: if you put the effort into developing your strength in this area, it will have a dramatic impact on your effectiveness as a leader and the results that you and your team create. We wish you great success in your journey to become significantly more inspirational.

Appendix 1

Further Research Information: The Multiplier Effect of Attributes

To help illustrate the impact of these attributes on inspiring others, we did an analysis on the level of employee commitment/engagement. Employee commitment/engagement was measured for each leader in our study. Based on that measure, we isolated those leaders who were at the ninetieth percentile or higher in their team's commitment/ engagement.

We then looked at leaders who were at the seventy-fifth percentile or higher on inspiring others. We found that 20 percent of the leaders with extraordinary employee commitment/engagement were in that cell.

We then looked at leaders who were at the seventy-fifth percentile or higher on enthusiasm/emotion. We found that only 16 percent of the leaders with extraordinary employee commitment/ engagement were in this cell.

Then we looked for the combined effect of being at or above the seventy-fifth percentile on both inspiring and using enthusiasm/ emotion. Compared to the 16 percent of those who possessed just one attribute, now 84 percent of the leaders who had extraordinary employee commitment/engagement had that combination of the two competencies. A leader who is only inspiring is good, just as a leader who is only enthusiastic is good. But a leader who is both inspiring and enthusiastic is extremely likely to be one of the top leaders in the organization.

We then looked at the impact of adding one additional competency to the mix. In this case, we looked at leaders who were above the seventy-fifth percentile on inspiring others, using enthusiasm/emotion, and one other competency (e.g., setting lofty goals, developing others, taking the initiative, or communication). With three combined competencies, the percentage of leaders who had extraordinary employee commitment/engagement ranged from 91 to 95 percent.

This demonstrates the synergy created by adding one strength to another. It appears that by using any three companion competencies, you will achieve approximately the same result.

Inspirational leadership is not about a single ingredient; it is all about the recipe. It comes about by combining ingredients. As you can see from our analysis, you can pick and choose which ingredients you want to use in your recipe. As you read through the book, select a few of the companion behaviors that fit your situation, that engage your passion, and that you believe would most benefit your organization.

Appendix 2

Frequently Asked Questions about Inspiration

We are asked the following questions with some frequency:

1. Is inspiring others the only competency that is necessary?
   No. In our research, we couldn't look at one competency isolated from others. We knew that leaders who were highly competent in inspiring others were also effective at other competencies. Consider the impact of a leader who worked very hard to be inspirational but who had a noticeable problem with integrity and honesty. If subordinates were aware of the leader's dishonesty, chances are they would not be inspired.

2. Does every leader need to be highly competent in inspiring others in order to be an effective leader?
   No. Inspiring others happens to have a substantial impact, but leaders can be very effective without having exceptional skills in this competency. It's not the only competency that will make a leader effective, but it is very influential. Inspiring others is not the only way to be an extraordinary leader, but it is an excellent option for those who are inclined to develop skill in this area.

3. Can everyone become extraordinary at inspiring others?

   No. The bad news is that to be extraordinary at a competency like inspiring others takes a combination of desire, practice, and talent, and not every person will be able to develop exceptional skills. The good news is that while we don't believe that everyone can be extraordinary, we do believe that anyone with a desire and a willingness to practice can be highly competent (e.g., seventy-fifth percentile) at this skill, and this generates a substantial impact.

Appendix 3

Full Text of Shakespeare's Version of Henry V's Speech to His Soldiers at Agincourt

Westmoreland: O, that we now had here
But one ten thousand of those men in England
That do no work today!

King: What's he that wishes so?
My cousin Westmoreland? No, my fair cousin.
If we are marked to die, we are enow
To do our country loss, and if to live,
The fewer men, the greater share of honor.
God's will! I pray thee wish not one man more.
By Jove, I am not covetous for gold,
Nor care I who doth feed upon my cost.
It yearns me not if men my garments wear;
Such outward things dwell not in my desires.
But if it be a sin to covet honor,
I am the most offending soul alive.
No, faith, my coz, wish not a man from England.
God's peace! I would not lose so great an honor

As one man more, methinks, would share from me
For the best hope I have. O, do not wish one more!
Rather proclaim it, Westmoreland, through my host
That he which hath no stomach to this fight,
Let him depart. His passport shall be made
And crowns for convoy put into his purse.
We would not die in that man's company
That fears his fellowship to die with us.
This day is called the feast of Crispian.
He that outlives this day and comes safe home
Will stand a-tiptoe when this day is named
And rouse him at the name of Crispian.
He that shall see this day and live old age
Will yearly on the vigil feast his neighbors,
And say, 'Tomorrow is Saint Crispian.'
Then will he strip his sleeve and show his scars,
And say 'These wounds I had on Crispin's day.'
Old men forget; yet all shall be forgot,
But he'll remember with advantages
What feats he did that day. Then shall our names,
Familiar in his mouth as household words—
Harry the King, Bedford and Exeter,
Warwick and Talbot, Salisbury and Gloucester—
Be in their flowing cups freshly remembered.
This story shall the good man teach his son.
And Crispin Crispian shall ne'er go by
From this day to the ending of the world,
But we in it shall be remembered—
We few, we happy few, we band of brothers.
For he today that sheds his blood with me
Shall be my brother. Be he ne'er so vile,
This day shall gentle his condition.
And gentlemen in England, now abed
Shall think themselves accursed they were not here,
And hold their manhoods cheap whiles any speaks
That fought with us upon Saint Crispin's day.

Endnotes

CHAPTER 1

1. There have been several articles and a small number of academic books written on the subject of charisma. Their conclusions differ widely. Their approach has been to define charismatic leaders as a unique category, possessed of several distinctive attributes and behaviors. We decided not to step into this debate, but instead to focus specifically on inspiration.

2. One author's background has been focused on the importance of behavior, and he has long argued that behavior always trumps emotion and attitude. A second author is a statistician and organizational psychologist by background. The third has extensive experience in professional selling, the acquisition of selling skills, and the development of sales leaders.

3. Max Weber, *The Theory of Social and Economic Organization,* translated by A. M. Henderson and Talcott Parsons (New York: Free Press and the Falcon's Bring Press, 1947).

4. We have heard of some university-based executive programs that have been experimenting with this topic, but nothing has been documented or published about it.

5. Belle Linda Halpern and Kathy Lubar, *Leadership Presence* (New York: Gotham Books, 2003).

CHAPTER 3

1. Hunter, Schmidt, and Judiesch, *Journal of Applied Psychology* 75, no. 1 (1990), pp. 28–42. Low-complexity jobs included clerical workers, laborers, file clerks, mail carriers, data entry clerks, and machine operators. Medium-complexity jobs included sales clerks, cooks, mechanics, claims adjusters, repairmen, and craftsmen. High-complexity jobs included physicians, dentists, attorneys, software engineers, and senior sales professionals.

2. Albert Bandura, "Organizational Applications of Social Cognitive Theory," *Australian Journal of Management,* December 1988.

3. Fred Luthans, "Investing in People for Competitive Advantage," *Organizational Dynamics* 33, no. 2 (2004), p. 20.

4. Martin Seligman, *Authentic Happiness* (New York: Free Press, 2002), p. 42.

5. Ibid., p. 40.

6. Martin Seligman, *Learned Optimism: How to Change Your Mind and Your Life* (New York: Free Press, 1999).

7. M. W. McCall Jr. and M. M. Lombardo, "Off the Track: Why and How Successful Executives Get Derailed," Technical Report No. 21 (Greensboro, N.C.: Center for Creative Leadership, 1983).

CHAPTER 4

1. John H. Zenger and Joseph Folkman, *The Extraordinary Leader: Turning Good Managers into Great Leaders* (New York: McGraw-Hill, 2002).

CHAPTER 5

1. Alan Wilkins, *Developing Corporate Character* (New York: John Wiley, 1989).

CHAPTER 6

1. Jack and Suzy Welch, "The Welchway," *BusinessWeek,* June 25, 2008, p. 86.

2. David Dorsey, "Andy Pearson Finds Love," *Fast Company,* August 2001, pp. 80–86.

3. Ibid., p. 86.

4. J. A. Conger and R. N. Kanungo, *Charismatic Leadership in Organizations* (Thousand Oaks, Calif.: Sage Publications, 1998).

5. A. P. Brief and H. M. Weiss, "Organizational Behavior: Affect in the Workplace," *Annual Review of Psychology* 53 (2002), pp. 279–307.

6. B. Shamir, R. J. House, and M. B. Arthur, "The Motivational Effects of Charismatic Leaders: A Self-Concept-Based Theory," *Organizational Science* 4 (1993), pp. 577–594; J. M. George, "Leader Positive Mood and Group Performance: The Case of Customer Service," *Journal of Applied Social Psychology* 25 (1995), pp. 778–794.

7. R. J. House, "A 1976 Theory of Charismatic Leadership," in J. G. Hunt and L. L. Larson (eds), *Leadership: The Cutting Edge* (Carbondale, Ill.: Southern Illinois University Press, 1977), pp. 189–207; Shamir, House, and Arthur, "Motivational Effects," *Organizational Science* 4:577–594.

8. Martin Seligman, *Authentic Happiness* (New York: Free Press, 2002), p. 40.

9. Conger and Kanungo, *Charismatic Leadership;* Remus Illies, Timothy Judge, and David Wagner, "Making Sense of Motivational Leadership: The Trail from Transformational Leaders to Motivated Followers, *Journal of Leadership and Organizational Studies,* September 2006.

10. George, "Leader Positive Mood," *Journal of Applied Social Psychology* 25:778–794.

CHAPTER 7

1. Joseph Carroll, Gallup News Service, September 6, 2007.

CHAPTER 9

1. David Dorsey, "Andy Pearson Finds Love," *Fast Company*, no. 49, 2001.

2. Kim Cameron, *Positive Leadership* (San Francisco: Berrett Koehler, 2008), p. 53.

3. Ibid.

4. M. Losada and E. Heaphy, "The Role of Positivity and Connectivity in the Performance of Business Teams: A Nonlinear Dynamic Model," *American Behavioral Scientist* 47, no. 6 (2004), pp. 740 765.

5. Cameron, *Positive Leadership*, p. 54.

6. C. Argyris, *Increasing Leadership Effectiveness* (New York: John Wiley, 1976).

7. Ruth Wageman, Debra A. Nunes, James A. Burruss, and J. Richard Hackman, *Senior Leadership Teams* (Boston: Harvard Business School Press, 2008), pp. 197–198.

8. Ibid., p. 199.

CHAPTER 10

1. Martin Seligman, *Authentic Happiness* (New York: Free Press, 2002), pp. 134–164.

2. Carol Dweck, *Mindset: The New Psychology of Success* (New York: Random House, 2006).

3. Guy Kawasaki, personal blog, guykawasaki.com.

4. Chris Argyris, *Flawed Advice and the Management Trap* (New York: Oxford University Press, 1999).

CHAPTER 11

1. David Nadler and Michael Tushman, *Competing by Design* (New York: Oxford University Press, 1997), p. 9.

2. John H. Zenger, Ed Musselwhite, Kathleen Hurson, and Craig Perrin, *Leading Teams: Mastering the New Role* (Homewood, Ill.: Business One Irwin, 1994), pp. 30–31.

CHAPTER 12

1. Regina Schrambling, "The Sharpest Knife in the Drawer," *Los Angeles Times,* March 8, 2006.

2. Wikipedia, "TRIZ."

3. Martin Seligman, *Authentic Happiness* (New York: Free Press, 2002), pp. 141–160.

4. Ibid., pp. 160–161.

CHAPTER 13

1. Our research on the impact that the best leaders can have is well documented in the book *The Extraordinary Leader: How Good Managers Can Become Great Leaders* (New York: McGraw-Hill, 2002).

Index

About the Authors

JOHN H. (JACK) ZENGER

John H. (Jack) Zenger is the cofounder
and CEO of Zenger Folkman, a professional services firm providing consulting, leadership development programs,
and implementation software for
organizational effectiveness initiatives.
Considered a world expert in the field
of leadership development, Jack is also a
highly respected and sought after
speaker, consultant, and executive coach.

Jack's career has combined entrepre-
neurial, corporate, and academic activi-
ties. In 1977 he cofounded Zenger-Miller and served as its president
and CEO until 1991. *The Wall Street Journal* named Zenger-Miller
one of the 10 best suppliers of executive development.

Because of his contributions to the field of leadership development and training, Jack was inducted into the Human Resources
Development Hall of Fame. His colleagues in the training industry

awarded him the "Thought Leadership Award" in 2007. Jack was honored as a distinguished citizen by the Stanford Area Council of Boy Scouts of America. Jack received a D.B.A. in business administration from the University of Southern California, an MBA from UCLA, and a BA in psychology from Brigham Young University.

Jack has authored or coauthored 50 articles on leadership, productivity, e-learning, training, and measurement. He is the coauthor of several books on leadership, including *Results-Based Leadership* (Harvard Business School Press, 1999), voted by SHRM as the Best Business Book in the year 2000, the bestselling *The Extraordinary Leader: Turning Good Managers into Great Leaders* (McGraw-Hill, 2002), and Handbook for Leaders (McGraw-Hill, 2004).

He is also a coauthor of books about teams, including the bestselling *Self-Directed Work Teams: The New American Challenge* (Irwin Professional Publishing, 1990), *Leading Teams* (Irwin Professional Publishing, 1993), and *Keeping Teams on Track* (Irwin Professional Publishing, 1996).

He and his wife, Holly, reside in Midway, Utah.

JOSEPH R. FOLKMAN

Joe Folkman is cofounder and president of Zenger Folkman, a firm that utilizes evidence-driven, strengths-based methods to improve organizations and the people within them. He is a respected authority on assessment and change, and an acclaimed keynote speaker at conferences and seminars the world over. His topics focus on a variety of subjects related to leadership, feedback, and individual and organizational change.

As one of the nation's renowned psychometricians, his extensive expertise focuses on survey research and change management. He has over 30 years of experience consulting with some of the world's most prestigious and successful organizations. His unique measurement tools are designed utilizing a database comprised of over a half million assessments on almost 50,000 leaders. Because these tools specifically address critical business results, facilitating development and change is the main focus of measurement efforts.

Joe's research has been published in several publications including the *Wall Street Journal*'s National Business Employment Weekly, *Training and Development* magazine, and *Executive Excellence*.

A distinguished expert in the field of survey design and data analysis, Joe consults with organizations large and small, public and private. He has had engagements with clients such as AT&T, Boeing, ConocoPhillips, CIBC, General Mills, Hunt Consolidated, Koch Industries, Marathon Oil, Nortel, Fidelity, First American, Reed-Elsevier, Safeway, Thomson Reuters, the U.S. Navy, UCSD, Wells Fargo, and Weyerhaeuser. The diversity of industries and business models has provided him with a powerful learning opportunity and an exceptional research base.

Joe holds a doctorate in social and organizational psychology, as well as a master's in organizational behavior from Brigham Young University. He is the author or coauthor of many books, including *Turning Feedback Into Change* (Executive Excellence, 1996), *Making Feedback Work* (Executive Excellence, 1998), *Employee Surveys That Make a Difference* (Executive Excellence, 1998), the bestselling *Extraordinary Leader: Turning Good Managers into Great Leaders* (McGraw-Hill, 2002), *The Handbook for Leaders* (McGraw-Hill, 2004), and *The Power of Feedback* (John Wiley, 2006).

Joe and his family reside at the base of the Wasatch Mountains in Orem, Utah.

SCOTT K. EDINGER

Scott K. Edinger is executive vice president at Zenger Folkman where he consults with Fortune 500 companies to initiate and implement large-scale performance improvement and leadership initiatives. Each year he works with hundreds of leaders to develop leadership talent and address the challenges of organizational change. Scott is recognized as an expert in helping organizations achieve measurable business results.

In his role, he tirelessly defines and refines Zenger Folkman's business and leadership strategies and does the same for the clients with whom he works. As an ambassador for the company, he is a popular keynote speaker at national conferences and has extensive experience working with some of the most prominent organizations in the world, including AT&T, Harvard Business School, Bank of America, Gannett, and the *Los Angeles Times.*

Having worked at one of the "Big Four" professional services firms, as well as various prominent training and consulting firms, Scott has extensive leadership, business development, consulting, coaching, and training experience. Moreover, as a result of having worked in this field in a variety of capacities (buyer, seller, and executive), Scott's experience is comprehensive and multidimensional.

Prior to joining Zenger Folkman, Scott worked for Huthwaite, Inc., as senior vice president of sales, where he led the company to record-levels of growth and success. He served the company in several roles, including vice president of international channel distribution and vice president of direct sales, and is also the author of Huthwaite's white paper, "Six Characteristics of World Class Sales Coaches."

Scott attended Florida State University where he received a BS in rhetoric and communication. He has contributed to publications such as *Leadership Excellence* and *Sales and Marketing Management*. He is also the coauthor of several white papers, including "How Extraordinary Leaders Double Profits."

Scott resides in Tampa, Florida, with his wife, Christine, and their family.

WHAT IS THE MOST POWERFUL PREDICTOR OF EXTRAORDINARY LEADERSHIP?

A leader's ability to inspire and motivate others.

Now that you've read *The Inspiring Leader* the question becomes, can the principles in this book really affect bottom-line profitability? Absolutely.

Zenger Folkman has created a unique training solution based on *The Inspiring Leader* that can drive significant, positive business outcomes. This program gives today's leaders a set of practical tools to help them develop the inspirational and motivational skills they need to increase employee engagement, retention, and productivity. And that, in turn, affects bottom-line profitability.

In addition, the team at Zenger Folkman has spent years studying thousands of leaders with one simple goal—to develop solutions that will help organizations and individuals improve leadership effectiveness. Our award-winning training solutions range from assessment tools and workshops to certification services and individualized coaching. Best of all, these solutions are designed with one thing in mind—to help organizations measurably improve leadership behavior and accelerate positive organizational change.

Ready to Learn More?

Call 801.705.9375
Visit www.zengerfolkman.com

 ZENGER | FOLKMAN